STANDBY

STANDBY

Sandy Broyard

Alfred A. Knopf *New York* 2005

THIS IS A BORZOI BOOK
PUBLISHED BY ALFRED A. KNOPF

Grateful acknowledgment is made to the following for permission to reprint
previously published material.

Alfred A. Knopf: Excerpts from "Esthétique du Mal,"
"Waving Adieu, Adieu, Adieu," and "The House Was Quiet
and the World Was Calm," from *The Collected Poems of
Wallace Stevens* by Wallace Stevens. Copyright © 1954
by Wallace Stevens and renewed 1982 by Holly Stevens.
Reprinted by permission of Alfred A. Knopf, a division
of Random House, Inc.

Copyright Clearance Center: Excerpt from "Unfinished
Business Keeps People Alive . . ." by Jay Carr, (*Boston Globe,*
February 23, 1992). Copyright © 1992 by Globe
Newspaper Co. (MA). Reprinted by permission of Globe
Newspaper Co. (MA) in the form of a trade book via the
Copyright Clearance Center.

Library of Congress Cataloging-in-Publication Data
Broyard, Sandy.
Standby / Sandy Broyard.
p.   cm.
ISBN 1-4000-4211-9 (alk. paper)
1. Grief.   2. Bereavement—Psychological aspects.
3. Death—Psychological aspects.   4. Broyard, Sandy.
5. Broyard, Anatole—Death and burial.   I. Title.
BF575.G7B758 2005
155.9'37'092—dc22
[B]   2004048383

Manufactured in the United States of America
First Edition

For

Todd and Bliss

learn to reach deeper
into the sorrows
. . . .
The still undanced cadence of vanishing.

GALWAY KINNELL

STANDBY

Embarking

After my husband died, I
began to write in a notebook, on scraps of paper, deposit slips,
anything handy. Putting words on paper was as necessary as
breathing. Having grief-driven words tucked away in my desk
allowed me to proceed with my life.

I am a therapist and each week I sit with people who are tor-
mented, confused, adrift in their lives, and I hear echoes of my
own story. They are entangled in and living their own painful
drama. Sometimes it is cumulative. For some, from early childhood on there have been endless cycles of deprivation, bad luck,
a mean world. Sometimes the onset has been sudden, tragic,
with an illness, loss of work, a death. I see them ensnared in the
jaws of an animal trap, the metal prongs clamped onto their
flesh and bone, while they bite and gnaw to free themselves.
When people first come into therapy, they don't understand that
the piercing pulling away from the source of agony is not the

answer. But rather, being still and using words, this is the medicine that slowly lessens the pain.

Listening to their distress has given me the courage to stay with my own pain, and as I have listened to them and been helped, it is my hope that these words will in turn help others.

The world of loss, the world of grief, of separation is a world of change, but change that is different from growth, from the normal, developmental flow of seasons, cells multiplying, learning, the transformations that keep things going. Loss is change that is abrupt, wrenching, change that leaves gaping holes, torn tendons, torn roots, jagged edges, a plant ripped out of the earth, a boulder moved aside for a highway. The open rawness demands a healing. But how to do that, how to proceed? It is not enough to restore the surface look of things. Oh, it's important to dress, to bathe, to comb your hair, mow the lawn, but the healing asks so much more of everything else you know how to do.

The troublesome part is this. Where is there a place or space for those of us who are engaged in this restorative process to be once more ourselves? The world that I found where I could most truly be myself, most truly feel myself was not with my friends—although they are good and patient friends who have listened and hugged and cried and laughed with me so generously—no, not with people, but rather by myself in a car. This is where I could cry without checking my tears to answer the phone, where I could scream obscenities, muse without interruption about my husband and my brother who had died, ponder my fears, mull over the absurdities of my life. And there in the standby line in Woods Hole waiting for the ferry to Martha's Vineyard I found the space, the place, the time to be truly with myself, aware of myself. Hard chunks of hard facts loosening, drifting onto the notebook page. Images to soften, or was it to release the bitter hurt of separation. A world, encapsulated like a snow globe. Soft liquid inside the car, its motion punctuated by the slow, deep breaths of two dogs sleeping, one next to me in the passenger seat, one in the back. Soft liquid with bits of myself lazily drift-ing up and out and then down around me. A consoling blanket of white, innocence returning, warming in its fragile way.

I have been patient working with these words. Why have I done this? Really, truthfully, it's because I do not have a choice. The alternative would be to numb out, to tune out, to change the dial of the radio that is tuned in to my particular history, my particular life. And I don't want to do that.

My parents and my boyfriend died, all unrelated deaths, when I was twenty. A year and a half later, episodes of uncontrol-lable shaking and sobbing began to happen without warning. A friend who witnessed one of these crises gave me a tranquilizer that I swallowed with a glass of wine. I was in Paris at the time. I passed out and a few hours later woke up, the dark feeling gone. That lesson went straight to my heart and brain. And for the next fifteen years I used that combination, not knowing that sedating myself only served to cement the torment to my bones.

Thirty-some years separates these early deaths from losing my husband, my brother, and a close friend in my fifties. With this second series of losses there were no small pills or magic potions to dilute or expunge the grief. The great sadness became words.

Final Days

September 2, 1990, Sunday.

6:10 p.m. Left for the Brigham.

6:40 p.m. Anatole admitted with a low temperature of 96.

6:50 p.m. Waiting for treatment in the emergency room, my husband says, "How can medical science and all their technology leave someone in their pain like this? Why do I have to wait?"

Five minutes later we are taken to a small examining room and joined by a fourth-year resident and a nurse. Anatole is given an injection of morphine.

"Right now it feels like the blood clots are birds trying to get out of their cage."

"I don't feel hopeless. I feel the proper equipment is in. We may be able to restore order and then I can function for a while."

Anatole has a body spasm. The sensation, he says, is like an excretion pushing through all his organs, only nothing happens. Perhaps he thinks he can push out the pain and the tumor.

"I think of them strangely enough as flowers, the little sources of pain. And when it goes away, they close up."

Our nurse, Jan, had been an army nurse and is now in the Reserves. She speaks with pride of her ability to handle extreme situations.

Anatole groggily asks the doctors for time. Time to finish his books. "I always had a writing block until I got cancer. Now everything flows."

These words take me into the darkness. My heart is trapped in itself as I remember Anatole trying to write in the hospital. He asked for paper and a pencil and could only make an illegible scrawl. I try to know or imagine how that felt for him. That's my profession, to be empathic. I need to have a sense of his dying. I want to smell and taste the agony of his dying, of how he was stripped of his faculties, the strength to walk, the ability to pee, to sit up without help, write a word on a page, have a mind free from the numbing of morphine. I am staying alive by staying with my husband's dying.

Now, some years later, what I remember most vividly is not my husband's pain and his struggle to survive but the long, tortured walk from where we parked the car to the ER. That was the last time Anatole walked. I loved his walk more than anything. When we first met, I was taking ballet at the Joffrey Studio in New York on Sixth Avenue and Tenth Street. I would have a place at the barre by an open window. The studio was on the second floor, and sometimes I would look down and see him walk by in the soft summer light of early evening, a warm Greenwich Village evening, his arms and legs swinging, slightly syncopated, back shifting right, left, right, and it would excite and please me to know that I knew this man, that I shared walks with this man.

Later that night of September 2, as I waited for our son Todd to pick me up, the hospital front entrance reminds me of an airport. What trip had just ended? The bag I travel with, a small flowered duffel, was now emptied of Anatole's glasses, toilet articles, a few books, two pencils, and a notebook. At home around midnight, while Todd and a friend were watching a video, I do laundry in the basement, crying, and then wash out a toilet. Earlier in the day, before going to the hospital, Anatole told me he had notes of how my face looked when I cried. Normally my Norwegian face, he said, looked like a cathedral of apricot stone, but when I cried it crumbled, the portals, the doors, my mouth breaking into pieces and falling apart.

Anatole was admitted to the Brigham Hospital because his kidneys were failing, and the cancer was breaking down internal tissue. Three days later he was transferred to the inpatient unit at the Dana Farber Cancer Institute across the street. He died on October 11. Through those final weeks I kept a notepad by my side so I could hold on to words that he could not write for himself.

"I've always had a problem in my life. Whenever I'm with my friends I feel responsible for the conversation."

"I'm cold. There's a draft here. No, it's cold inside around the heart. That's from Eliot."

My husband says these things while we're waiting in a hospital corridor after a session of X-rays. He's lying on a gurney, and I'm standing near his shoulders, shielding his face from the eyes of people walking by.

Some days later we have this conversation.

"Why are they making such a big fuss over me in this hospital?"

"Who?"

"The women."

"They always have."

"But why now? I'm skinny, shrunken, invisible. I'm practically invisible."

And at another time.

"My reality weakens so she doesn't hurt me as much. Who is she, the analyst?"

Perhaps Anatole in the fog of morphine and his illness was remembering lines from his favorite poet, Wallace Stevens.

> *The softest woman,*
> *Because she is as she was, reality,*
> *The gross, the fecund, proved him against the touch*
> *Of impersonal pain. Reality explained.*
> *It was the last nostalgia: that he*
> *Should understand. That he might suffer or that*
> *He might die was the innocence of living.*
>
> Esthétique du Mal

Eleven days before he died Anatole and Dr. Patterson, the attending intern, talk about the possibility of going home. Anatole apologizes for his impatience, saying that his life is his writing and he hadn't made the effort and arrangements to do that work in the hospital. Anatole explains that writers need their special nooks to work in and perhaps he should have made one in the hospital. Dr. Patterson assures him that up to now he'd been too sick to do that.

The next day I see Dr. Ho, a young doctor who had been involved in Anatole's treatment in his previous hospitalization. I remind him about the time he sat next to Anatole on the bed. Anatole asked him about getting the pain under control. Dr. Ho assured him that this could be done. Then my husband asked Dr. Ho if he could take care of his soul. Anatole was sitting up in bed, Dr. Ho next to him. The two men side by side, hip to hip and shoulder to shoulder. The young doctor was quiet. He said nothing, but he stayed there. He didn't pull away. He didn't try to fill the silence or change the subject, even though he clearly did not know what to say. The two men sat for some moments breathing quietly. Dr. Ho tells me that Anatole had said to him that his illness had made him feel like a child again with emptiness inside, but within the emptiness a spark remained.

On October 8 our friends Suzy and Hugh from New York come up for the day. This is how they're spending their twenty-ninth wedding anniversary. Ours, Anatole's and mine, our twenty-ninth anniversary is the following Sunday.

We had met on a subway train, the Lexington Avenue IRT. At the Fourteenth Street station we walked onto the same car and held on to the same pole. He asked me what class I was taking at the New School. He'd seen me leave the Twelfth Street building. I replied, a Chinese Art History course taught by a professor with an unintelligible accent. Anatole said he was teaching a class on Sociology and Popular Culture. I laughed and said, Yes, I'd noticed that class and thought, How typical of the New School to be so trendy. We got off at Grand Central Station and had a brief drink at the bar in the Vanderbilt Hotel. He went off to meet friends and I took a train back to Mamaroneck, where I was living with my sister and her husband.

Eight months later we were married in the Greenwich Village townhouse that belonged to the mother of a close college friend. The minister we'd found taught drama at Union Theological Seminary. Friends and family, about fifty in all, ate deviled eggs and wedding cake from a local bakery. During the ceremony Anatole and I both noticed that the minister had dandruff on his shoulders, clearly visible on his black vestments.

Suzy and I share memories of courtship, early marriage, babies. Hugh sits next to Anatole, who is mostly unconscious now, reading the Sunday *Times* while holding his hand. Suzy looks at her husband sitting there with his dying friend and tells me that Hugh hadn't been able to do that with his own father.

Our daughter, Bliss, comes at seven. Her face is pained as she looks at her father. She went to Walden Pond today with a college friend, Robin, and worked on a story. Todd, our son, here for the weekend, went back to Connecticut, where he lives and works. A week ago Wednesday Anatole put his arms around me. Tuesday he kissed me, but his last smile was for his nurse, Myra.

As I remember my husband's final smile, I also imagine him as a baby in his mother's arms, eyes attuned, and then the first shy smile, the small movement of cheek and mouth and eyes that connects parent and child. We are held, we are seen, we are loved, and we smile.

There is a photograph of Bliss and her father. She is eleven months and is seated on her father's lap at a kitchen table next to a window, holding a piece of an English muffin in one hand. Her head is tilted up. She is looking into her father's eyes. His head bows toward hers. Morning sun lights her face. Both father and daughter are smiling.

I'm not a photographer, but over the years of pointing and shooting occasionally the film captures a moment that contains what I knew and felt to be there at the time. The solid happiness of a child, your child on your husband's lap, smiling up at him, sunshine on her face at the beginning of a new day, a day when the world will be sunny and warm, inviting one to play, to work, to learn.

When I look at this photo or just think about it I get teary. Being the mother, the wife, being part of something so fine and alive as this smile of father and daughter, this moment of trust and contentment is a thing quite simply glorious.

There was no camera for my husband's final smiles, but I remember them clearly. His smile for Bliss or Todd as they entered his room or left, saying, "I love you." His smiles for me as I would lean over him and kiss his brow at midnight before going home to sleep. Anatole's ability to smile remained when he could no longer speak.

Now I think about the first and last smiles of my husband's life. They appear as luminous parentheses to all the words he spoke and wrote. The first smile. Yes, it's me and you're my mom. And at the end, the last glancing smile, a brief surfacing of final contact, more amorphous than the first, a smile to embrace all his years, all his experience, eyes gazing up to the caring face of his nurse.

Gwindale remembers Anatole saying, "Will I like it there? Some men don't like music." Gwindale, the wife of Anatole's closest friend is a classical pianist. She adds that this was not said with fear or despair but rather with a sense of pragmatism.

October Through April

The amazing thing about grief is that it doesn't hurt all the time.

People tell me to keep busy, not to be alone, which at first was necessary. Now I can risk sitting by myself with my thoughts. My one feeling is that I want my husband. I want him beside me as I walk down the street. I long for his impatience. I miss his knowledge, his memory, his ability to quote passages from prose and poetry. I miss his taste, his pronouncements about books, writers, movies, his likes and dislikes. I miss our partnership. But most of all I miss the happiness of our companionship.

When Anatole was sick I had to function each day putting fear and anxiety aside. That habit persisted in the weeks after his death. Now I'm beginning to fall apart.

Walking back from Harvard Square I am filled with sadness. I begin to cry. There's an intimacy to it. I compare these tears to tears shed during the marriage when I felt I wasn't being understood, wasn't acknowledged, or when I was angry at Anatole for his pigheadedness. There was always an intensity and intimacy because there was an *other*, a *he*. Now here on the street, walking down Mass Ave., my tears again bind me to Anatole. As I cry, I wonder if I am crying over my loss, or am I crying for Anatole, for his loss of his life? A friend wrote a week after he died, "My sadness is mainly at what Anatole is missing, his enjoyment and pleasure in friends."

With Anatole's death I begin to sense that I have less of an investment in my own ego. There's a paradox here. As I begin to find out about my ability to live by myself I'm less interested in my own narrow satisfactions.

While he was ill Anatole kept a notebook in which he jotted down his thoughts in preparation for the articles he wrote about his illness for the *New York Times* and for a book, never finished, on the same subject. He had thought of calling it *Critically Ill.* He wanted to do justice to cancer as a momentous experience. He wanted the book to be personal, a narrative, a love story.

"Our sexual life and passion is not isolated in the genitals."

Nor is it bound only to physical touch. After twenty-nine years of marriage it's part of the whole fabric of a relationship. Perhaps it continues with these words, these memories, this effort to tell the pain of separation.

"Language, speech and stories are the most effective way to keep our humanity alive."

"With my father's death, cancer started me as a writer 40 years ago."

With my husband's death, grief is pulling me into myself, where I am finding solace with pencil and paper and words.

When I go to the North Cambridge post office the closest parking spaces are by the side of Long's Funeral Home, where Anatole's body was taken after he died. I imagine him there, alone in an empty room, dark, cold.

I startle because only now do I realize that it didn't occur to me to bring him clothes to be cremated in. I sit here losing my breath as I become desperate to know if sheets or drapes or coverings of any sort are used for the dead who are waiting to be burned. Why didn't I think to ask?

Anatole's body was still him, and he needed, more so then than at any other time of his life, what he himself could not ask for but what he would have asked for if he had been able to. If he could have, he would have called me from the funeral home saying that he wanted his blue striped shirt, the one with long sleeves that he'd gotten on the Vineyard, and to bring his old khakis, since they had a smaller waist and he'd lost weight, then tan socks and his Cole Haan docksiders. He would have said that he'd decided on a casual look for his cremation, since it was taking place in the Gothic Chapel in the Mount Auburn Cemetery in Cambridge. The weather was sunny and warm, a Saturday morning, early, at 8 a.m. He would have wanted to wear for his final appointment on earth what he would have worn had he and I been taking a walk that day. Anatole was a casual guy, but clothes and comfort were important to him. I recoiled from the skin and tissue I knew so well when his breath stopped and his mind stilled. His body was no longer him, yet sitting here tonight I know I was wrong. The still, cold body in Long's Funeral Home continued to be my husband, and it is terrible that I did not bring him his clothes.

I need to go back and consider these things because it wasn't possible at the time. The moments and events and details are too important to let disappear and fade away.

As I read for the first time Tolstoy's *The Death of Ivan Illich,* I see Anatole, not Tolstoy's hero, I hear about Anatole not from his bed at the Dana Farber hospital but from a room in Moscow.

"Something terrible, new and so important was taking place in him and he alone knew of it."

"We sick people probably often ask inconvenient questions."

"At the bottom of his heart Ivan Illich knew he was dying. He simply did not grasp it."

"Pain rivets Ivan Illich's attention to death. Arguing dispelled thoughts of death. It was a lie that if Ivan Illich kept quiet and followed the doctor's orders he would be better."

"And he had to live thus, on the edge of the precipice alone."

This is a time to get to know my husband in another way. There is distance and quiet now. Where was he? How was his death for him? I remember his eyes, as Tolstoy writes of Ivan Illich, *"shining with terror and hope."*

How do other people die? Did I or we, family and friends, do Anatole a disservice? Did we help him to have the kind of death he would have wished or did we botch it? Did we acknowledge his dying as fully as he would have liked? All this haunts me. I'm afraid to look as I know I must.

What about my efforts to get Anatole to eat? I would prepare a fourteen-grain cereal, moistened the night before with apple juice, and remind Anatole to take the pain meds before eating so that the nausea would be less. He would get halfway through a meal and then lie down on the love seat so as not to vomit. I'm confused. Did I make a mistake? Did I misread the discomfort and sickness of the Gonzalez treatment?

The final months of his life Anatole tried an alternative cancer approach offered by Dr. Nicolas Gonzalez of New York. The protocol was pancreatic enzymes, vitamin and mineral supplements, 160 pills a day together with a diet of organic foods. The enzymes made Anatole very sick. We saw this as the price for a cure. But were the nausea and vomiting really the symptoms of dying?

Another hard day. Grief is essentially a solitary activity. I didn't call anyone because I wanted to stay with and not crawl out of the pain. I'm scattered, overwhelmed, forgetful, unfocused, constantly anxious, and unable to concentrate. I'm eating too much sugar. Fran, a friend who's a therapist, says this is normal. I'm exhausted. I woke at five-thirty this morning. Stayed in bed until seven. Finally got some bills paid.

Went to the movies with Ann McGhee. We tried Cambridge and Fresh Pond but the lines were too long. Ended up at West Newton and saw *C'est la vie*. As we were driving from town to town I kept noticing funeral parlors. In Newton after the movie we walked across a bridge that spans the Mass Pike. I remembered Marie, with whom I'd worked ten years ago. She had tried to kill her herself by jumping onto the New England Thruway from an overpass after her husband died. Badly injured, she survived.

On my bookshelf there is a small fragile New Testament, its leather binding thin and flaking at its corners. My father had carried it with him when he was in France during the First World War, driving an ambulance for the American Field Service. In the flyleaf there is an inscription dated December 17, 1916. "Verdun, the city that has held out against and overcome her enemies. If only all men would do the same against their enemies." Late one night two and a half years later in Canton, China, where he was living and working for an American bank my father wrote again in the flyleaf: "Be a man and hold fast that which is good." I don't know what he was struggling with, but I recognize the voice of a weary, weakened soul.

I haven't prayed since Anatole died. Last Easter I prayed all day, at church in the morning and through to the evening. I have nothing to say to God now. I don't blame him. I no longer have a connection with him. I don't trust him.

When I don't cry I am beyond tears in a place where there is no emotion. The degree to which I miss Anatole is so great that tears and sadness have no relationship to the void that is in my life now. Tears are for something specific. Losing my husband is like losing who I am. It is losing the texture, the denseness, the three-dimensional quality of my life. Now I am only flat. I am not even me.

Tomorrow is Easter. A celebration for a resurrection. Yet I remain prone.

In Anatole's study I come across a book, *The Illness Narratives,* written by Arthur Kleinman, who is both an anthropologist and a psychiatrist. Dr. Kleinman had asked Anatole to come talk to his class at Harvard about the experience of illness. In the book Anatole had made a mark beside this sentence.

"An illness narrative makes sense and gives value to the experience." Perhaps with these words a grief narrative will do the same.

Time may ease but it doesn't erase loss. Loss stays with you. I still miss my parents and Ben, my college boyfriend, who died at twenty-two. I miss all my animals, Smudge, Pepper, Bounce, Becky, Hicks and Daisy and Benny. Losses are like crustaceans or barnacles that you accumulate through life. They slow you down.

This Saturday I went to Newport for the day with a college friend to tour the mansions. I couldn't tolerate the possible loss of an old black glove. It had fallen out of the car in the parking lot and I walked back a half mile to retrieve it. It would have been too much to have lost both a husband and a black leather glove.

My car has a flat tire. Will flat tires always remind me of Anatole's operation the month before he died? That afternoon his bladder had burst, and I had to make the decision about whether to let him die then or give him a few more weeks of life by repairing the internal hemorrhaging. After he had been stabilized by a crisis team of doctors and nurses, I was allowed to see him. He was lying on a bed that was a board, his feet higher than his head, his face ashen, like a dying Christ figure in a sixteenth-century painting where the artist was working with perspective and immediacy.

His doctor and a nurse led me to the visitors' waiting room and closed the door. I sat on a couch opposite the doctor. He told me that my husband would be dead in a few hours. Bands of sunlight stretching across the rug held my eyes steady, but my mouth opened wide in a long scream that had no sound, and then I swallowed and looked up. The doctor said that an operation might give him a bit more time. I couldn't let Anatole die that day.

An ambulance was ordered to transport him across the street to Brigham and Women's Hospital. He was in no shape to be rolled through the long corridors and skyways that connected the two hospitals. When I asked, the surgeon said, yes, I could accompany my husband in the ambulance. He would do the same if his wife were ill. I stayed with Anatole until he was taken into the operating room. He had regained consciousness by then. The last thing he said to me before the operation as I leaned over to kiss him was "You have whimsical taste in men." I had said, "I love you." The date was September 10. The operation began at midnight, and at four in the morning we learned that he would have more time. Todd, Bliss, and I walked over to Todd's car on Brookline Ave. There was a flat tire. Todd began to change it. I remember the emptiness of the street, no cars, a lone man on a bike with a helmet.

Just now as I walked back into the house I thought of how Anatole was at that point. We were just glad that he was alive, still breathing. But where was he? Where was his brain? Could he still dream? Where was his soul? His body had been cut and parted and patched and sewn. I never asked the surgeon what he saw when he opened up my husband.

I don't want to forget Anatole's suffering. As I hold on to the memories of the most intimate moments of our love life, I also want to know these other details. For his sake I don't want to erase the sharp edges of his purgatory. I am his amanuensis. My job is to testify, to report, to tell others about his suffering and the ravages of the cancer. What *it* did. Why *it* was so terrible.

I don't know what this past year was like for the children. I can't place them last summer. It was as if Anatole and I were on an iceberg together. I only remember Janie Hitchcock, a friend from New York, calling. Otherwise we were cut off.

Our last walks together were in early August, to David Kantor's, a therapist and friend that we spoke to a few times who lived a block away. And we went to Fresh Pond, but Anatole was only comfortable with a few steps up a hill to a bench. I kept hoping he could go farther. I assumed that by wanting something it would be possible.

When I am thinking about Anatole and his illness, I feel I've come back to myself, that I've returned to my life. Escaping doesn't work.

Thoughts are forcing me to write. If I don't write, I don't know where these memories will go or what will happen to them. They are too important to not pay attention to, these images of how my husband died six months ago. When they come back to me, they take my breath away. The pain that Anatole endured makes me want to scream. He suffered so much, this man that I had loved and continue to love, a man I had lived with for thirty years, who is the father of my two children, who was my provider, my home port, a man whom I never got tired walking toward.

What do I do with these memories? Do I recount the horror of his physical death? I can allude to it, but I can't tell it all. There are some things in life that are either so beautiful or so brutal that they must be kept to oneself as if they were sacred to the self. Perhaps they are. Moments that go beyond your imagination, beyond your expectations of what you'd assumed you were capable of doing or feeling, moments of either great joy or great horror.

Anatole wrote, "There must be something beyond love. I want to get there."

Could it be that when I recall these things that I shall never tell anyone, stories that are only for myself, that then I will be in that place beyond love?

I continue to look through Anatole's notebooks, and there I find a correspondence between his illness and my grief.

"the aloneness of the critically ill"

"a solitude as haunting as a de Chirico painting"

Anatole had written in an essay about books on illness that there are many that tell you about the waking hours but "not much about daydreams and fantasies and how the illness transforms you." He also felt that with these subjects there was sometimes a tendency to be too pious, to avoid the ugly, to tiptoe through the sick man's room so as not to disturb. He wrote, "I want to wrap my story in the specific."

We are waiting for the results of some X-rays at the Brigham, which will tell us if the cancer has spread to the bones. We watch a doctor with a bag of popcorn give another patient good news about her tests. We continue to wait for our results. Finally the doctor comes back with the popcorn still in his hands to say that the previous X-rays can't be found, which means that he has no baseline, nothing to compare with. We get no news, no sense. We are too numb to think of any questions that might give us some information. The popcorn bag seems like a shield for the doctor to hide behind. Has he really seen something bad and does not want to be the one to tell us? That's what it seems like.

·   ·   ·

Last weekend I was dancing the lindy with Bliss at a friend's eightieth birthday. I couldn't remember how Anatole did the lindy. I lost the steps and they suddenly seemed very important— the in-between quick syncopated steps, but then tonight as I was going to sleep I remembered.

Left, left, right, left. Then twice as fast. Right, left, right.

Specifics

Just before he died Anatole didn't need to have his teeth brushed. He'd had no food in over a month—or practically none. Sometimes I think that he starved to death, that it wasn't cancer at all. Like the stories just now coming out of Chinese orphanages in Shanghai of the dying rooms. Children tied down to straw pallets, given no nourishment, and left to die because they were hard to handle or deformed or needed too much care, or just because they weren't appealing.

Near the end there were swabs and a solution for his mouth to wash away the scabs, the nurses recommending one brand over another as if it were a more efficient mop for floors. Amazing how it is possible to normalize the most grotesque activities. Imagine swabbing scabs and blood out of the mouth of your husband of twenty-nine years. Out of a mouth that no longer can talk. Only rattled breaths. Amazing that I could remain sane and not throw myself out the window or jump off a bridge. I understand now how widows in India can throw themselves onto their husband's funeral pyre. That is more reasonable than standing calmly next to a mechanized hospital bed and inserting sterile pink swabs into the mouth of your lover. The care that is needed as the end of life approaches is an inner sanctum of mysteries, of rituals not spoken about. The transfers to change sheets, the washing, the turning. It must all be done so carefully. The thread of life is so fragile at this point. And yet I kept hoping for a reversal, hoping for the impossible. I kept on hoping until a week before he died.

Dr. Eberlein, the surgeon who'd operated on Anatole, who'd given me his home phone number as well as those of hospital and office in case I had questions, Dr. Eberlein came to tell me that my husband was dying. Going out into the hallway, holding on to my hands, he said those words. He knew I was falling, but he also knew that if he held both my hands and wrists, I could continue to stand. And he knew as I didn't know that I must stay upright. He talked me through the transition from hope to knowing that Anatole was dying.

A Tiffany catalogue comes in the mail. It brings to mind an afternoon with Anatole in the Brigham last August. I left him and took the Green Line into Copley Place and went to Tiffany to get a wedding present for Suzy and Hugh's daughter, Wendy. I bought silver starfish earrings for Bliss on an impulse. Anatole thought I had been extravagant and wanted me to return them. A few days later we gave them to Bliss on her twenty-fourth birthday. By then Anatole had been moved to the Dana Farber and was barely conscious because of the pain medications. Gwindale had made a birthday cake and dinner. Her husband, Mike, brought the food to the hospital. Two of Bliss's friends came by. We sang a muffled "Happy Birthday" so as not to disturb Anatole or the patients in nearby rooms. After the others left, Mike talked to his buddy but Anatole couldn't talk back. Just a week before, Anatole had told us the story about chairs flying through the air like butterflies at a dance hall in Spanish Harlem.

Walking down Craige Street in Cambridge, I stop to look at an overgrown garden choked with tall ornamental grasses and masses of lupine. There is a stand of twelve slender birch trees crowded into a rug-sized space by the driveway. Neighbors have commented about the unruliness of the plan. Someone is weeding. I speak to her. She designed the garden and offers to give me a tour. I step inside the fence, and she leads me along a slender path that weaves through the jungle. From inside, the garden becomes magical. The street a few feet away is lost to sight and sense. Shrubs and small trees are underplanted with ground covers, ferns and perennials, all placed randomly as if by birds that had dropped seeds. At each bend of the path there is a surprise, something unexpected. The path is a journey through possibilities. Finally one comes to a small sunken square of grass, stone-lined, like a small pool, but instead of the ripple and reflection of water, there for contemplation is an evenly cropped green that makes you realize you'd never truly seen the beauty of grass before.

On impulse I tell the designer that my husband has died and I want to work on my garden. The Wendell Street house had a deep back yard, forty-five by ninety feet. She gives me her card.

A few days later we meet. I tell her how as a family we had always danced together. In college Bliss wrote a story that ended with a daughter and father at a wedding doing a slow drag across the dance floor. I tell her about the nights before our kids went off to college. As a family we went out dancing. I talk about all the dancing we've been robbed of by Anatole's death. The designer suggests that the new garden be a place for dancing. Making a space for our family's dance could be an expression of what we are now. The loss will be given shape. A landscape, or to be more precise, a yardscape, can be created out of the void.

At the end of the meeting I ask how much this transformation would cost. I had naïvely thought perhaps $2,000. The designer says in the neighborhood of $20,000. I pay her hourly consultation fee and am pleased to have had at least a vision for the future.

Later that day I find a box of my summer clothes. I haven't seen them in two years. I didn't even know they were missing.

Whatever sense I have for the future lies outside of myself. A new garden, a new job. Those things I can see, but inside of myself and my home there is chaos. Does the mess and disorder continue as a by-product of my internal fracturing? Is loss about picking up one sock and walking twenty-two steps to another room and placing it on my son's bed? Perhaps I should just concentrate on lost socks. Spend a week combing the house for mismatched socks. Would a week be enough?

When we moved to Cambridge I started a small psychotherapy practice, seeing clients one day a week at a nearby office. I kept up with it through Anatole's illness and his death. Continuing to work has been a support for me, but at times a session can be painful, as was last night's. The client talked about her brother's recent death, describing how the family came together in her brother's room, encapsulating in their final words all the poignancies of their life together. As she talked I realized I, or rather we, Anatole and myself, hadn't said goodbye.

Today I'm thinking about all the times I left for the Vineyard alone in the spring and fall to open and close our summer home. It was the only place I ever went alone. The car would be packed, the boxes and animals tucked in together, and there would be four or five stages of last-minute reminders and goodbyes. Anatole would readjust the boxes in the back of the car for better weight distribution. A trip back to the kitchen would produce a ham-and-cheese sandwich for on-the-road eating. Back to the house, and Anatole would reappear with a jug of water for the dogs. We liked these long disjointed partings. Then why couldn't we say goodbye as Anatole was dying? Perhaps, it just occurs to me now, he needed to keep us with him, close to him, and he feared the distance, the aloneness, if we'd begun our goodbyes. We were there with him holding his hand, sitting in the room, talking to one another, keeping life going. How could he say goodbye? He didn't want to leave.

Saw the movie *Truly, Madly, Deeply.* A painful experience. I knew it would be. It's about a woman whose boyfriend dies suddenly and then returns in the flesh. She meets someone else and has to decide whether to stay with the dead or the living. As I work with Anatole's words, collecting his writings on illness and death, I stay with him. I attempt to think about another man in my life but that's all I can do. I can have adolescent fantasies, but I feel surrounded by negative ions. When I'm around another man it's as if Anatole is away on an extended trip and I am doing some socializing in the meantime.

Tonight I went through some of his clothes that were in the hall chest. As I sorted and folded the socks, I thought of how those fibers had been next to his skin, of how his body weight had pressed and compacted the wool and cotton against the inner sole of his shoe as he stood or walked or paced. The silk socks and thermal underwear were new purchases. The illness had left him chilled.

I'm dusting and vacuuming those parts of the house that I can get at, that are not obstructed by boxes, piles of random clothes, unidentifiable objects. Disorder has engulfed the house. I'm converting the basement into a one-bedroom apartment and raising the roof on the third floor so a full bathroom can be added there. While Anatole was sick we had tried to sell this house but couldn't. He had wanted to move to a house with larger rooms. He said he needed more space to wrestle with the cancer. We actually made offers on two other houses, but our house didn't sell. The real estate agents thought this was because there were only one and a half baths. Knowing that this is too much house for just myself and I must one day leave, I'm trying to make it more salable. Everything that had been stored in the basement is now in the dining room or the upstairs hallway or has been tucked randomly into any available corner.

Bliss and I did make some headway and got the attic crawl spaces cleaned out and a few boxes and items stored away. We went through three large bags of Anatole's clothes. We separated those we wanted from stuff to give to Goodwill and then made a separate pile for friends to go through. Anatole was very particular about the way he dressed. He chose his clothes carefully and wore them well. The shirts and sweaters still contain his anima. I can't give his flannel nightshirts away. Memories of Anatole sitting in bed drift back, reading before going to sleep, the soft cotton against the skin I knew so well. I am wearing his shirts and sweaters, but it doesn't occur to me to wear his nightshirts. Instead I tear them up so they can be cleaning rags. Using his nightshirts to dust tables, polish chests, then the intimacy continues. Except for the five years when I worked full-time, I've always done my own housework. I like taking care of the familiar surfaces of my life. Tonight I'll clean.

At nine I stop, thinking I'll watch *Masterpiece Theatre.* Todd and his friend Dave are watching a basketball game downstairs. I go to Todd's room to turn on his set. It's not connected to an antenna. There is only static on the screen. I stumble into my bedroom crying. If Anatole were alive we'd be watching *Masterpiece Theatre* together. There would be a rhythm, a balance, an ebb and flow of relatedness. Who am I related to now? There are the two children and the four animals. And I'm still very much with Anatole, with his work, his memory, his presence, or rather with his lack of presence. He is simply not here, and I am alone. I feel alone. I sleep with a dog crate on my bed, for we have just gotten a new puppy, an eight-week-old black Lab whom we've named Player.

The only time my aloneness is tolerable is when I'm dancing. When I move I am full. I have meaning to myself. I realize there is no way I could sustain a relationship with anyone else. I can only flirt with fantasies, which is what I did when Anatole was alive. I also realize that when Anatole was very sick and I knew that his cancer could kill, I thought that it would happen in a number of years, not months. How could he slip away so quickly?

I remember him sitting in the small wing chair in the living room talking to the hospice volunteer. He had just finished the last review he was to write. He was so gallant, so charming to the young man who was going to be his babysitter while I left the house for errands and a run. They talked about literature and life in Cambridge. You would have thought that our visitor was a young writer. That was on a Monday. On Tuesday he was in the hospital. There were clots in his urine and a new kind of pain. The horrible thing about illness is that it is so physical. Tissue breaks down. The body disintegrates, it fails, it mutinies. When clots appear you can't breathe them away or wish or meditate them away. Was this the beginning of Anatole's bladder breaking down? Why do we assume we can trust anything in this world? Why?

Now I wonder if there is a connection between those clots and the debris that fills this house. Is my life breaking down? Does a point get reached where there is no return, where there can be no possibility of healing, no restoration or return to order? Beyond that point there is only death and disintegration, a coming apart of what we assume and have come to trust will stay intact because that is the nature of bodies and houses and their contents. But if you go too far, can you come back?

While I was painting the pantry shelves that Todd made for the basement apartment kitchen I heard a Scarlatti flute-and-harpsichord sonata on WBUR. Anatole played the same recording in his Twelfth Street apartment when I first met him. The music takes me back to the empty rooms with their gleaming wood floors and no furniture except for a bed, a table, and a chair and sheer nylon curtains at open windows looking onto the trees of the back yard. I think of a forty-year-old man and the music he chooses to listen to. The bouncy, dancey, lyrical flute melody catches his spirit, his playfulness, his "catch me if you can" quality. It was as if with all his women he was playing tag.

Eight months and four days since Anatole died. I notice his Tiffany watch, the one I gave him for his seventieth birthday, two months and twenty-five days before he died, the watch that I had hoped, had assumed would mark years, not days or weeks as it did. I don't remember when we took it off his arm. Was it when we knew he could no longer tell time because of loss of brain function, or was it because he could no longer see? I can't remember the last time he wore his glasses. What was the last thing he saw? The nurses kept saying that hearing is the last sense to go. What happens with sight? Do eyes lose their ability to focus? Does the world become a blur? I started to wear the Tiffany watch after my own had stopped. No time to get a battery. Then after a few months, that watch also stopped. Now I wear a $15 digital watch from 47th Street Photo that I got eight years ago that never stops and never needs a replacement battery. The only problem is that I can't read the time without my glasses.

Eight months and four days. I am alone and empty in a way that I wasn't before. It's as if I'm beginning to wake up to the reality of my new life and it frightens me. Having the new puppy is a distraction, but it also reminds me that the fullness of our family will never again be the way it was. There is a thinness now. I don't have it in me to provide the food, the order, the cleanliness, the assurance that home is a stable place where you come and get refueled. I am tottering on the edge of my own existence and toying with all sorts of catastrophes.

I cry every day now. It's not that I mind all the crying. The wetness and feelings will pass. What troubles me is the brooding sadness. It feels like a dampness creeping into my life, accompanied by mold. I fear that the edges of the shapes that are familiar to me will turn limp and musty green. The house looks as if it has gotten beyond the point of sorting and arranging. Comments about the Collyer brothers are no longer funny. The upheaval is too real. Am I a collaborator? Do I languish in this state of grief, of mess, of being lost? The ongoing grief, is it a way of being loyal to Anatole, staying close to him by sinking into this mire?

These are my thoughts at eight on a Saturday night. I'll return to the basement and continue painting, trudging forward, slowly.

Ashes

When my husband died he left me all his words. Forty years of book reviews, short stories, travel articles, literary essays, unfinished manuscripts about his illness, about his youth in Greenwich Village. When we got married and had the prenuptial meeting with the minister, I asked for "till death do us part" to be taken out of the ceremony. I don't know why. It just seemed to make sense that two people who loved one another enough to get married could not be separated.

Death has not parted us. I am working more intimately with him now than when he was alive. There was so much busyness when he was alive. With his absence there is a possibility of a different kind of understanding. I have put my work in the background. Finishing Anatole's is now my occupation. The first project is to bring together his writings about death and illness. A few months before he died he signed a contract for a book on illness. He had written three articles for the *New York Times* about his sickness and was going to expand these essays. He didn't get the time to work on this, nor did he mention his thoughts about the evolution of the book. After five months of my efforts the manuscript is almost complete. It's a combination of essays, reviews, and a piece of fiction. Ruminations on existence and nonexistence.

I sit in the living room and work on the epilogue. I've been putting this last bit off. When I finish I will be leaving a certain part of this experience, and I'm afraid of putting distance between myself and Anatole's death. I am still hovering over his face at Dana Farber, hoping for more words, more meaning, some sign from him, something. I imagine him saying "I love you. I love life. I love my children. I've had a good time. I don't want to die. I'm dying. I won't die."

What could he have said that I, that we, didn't already know? Anatole detested banalities. It infuriated him when I would answer a question with an obvious response. Sometimes I used to purposely tease him with a simple answer. After thirty years of being together there is a bit of mind reading, a filling in of words, shortcut communication. Anatole always said I should know him well enough to know what he meant. Can I assume that he believed that I knew where he was and what he was thinking when he was dying? As I ask these questions I realize that we, Anatole and I, believed that he was not dying, that he was living, that he was choosing to live while he could talk. He was choosing to be fey and flirtatious. Catch me, catch my drift if you can. He continued to surprise, to do offbeats, to syncopate his responses, to say interesting, not maudlin things, to be himself. So he never said "I don't want to die." All he said was "I'm a very sick man." And we, his family and friends, said, "Yes." We nodded in agreement, our eyes moist, for we didn't want to lose him.

As I work on the epilogue, I find once again the pleasure of sinking into words. The simplicity of it. Myself and my thoughts, mulling all these things over. There's an intimacy in writing, a sense of being in the right place, of having won out against the sadness and the intrusiveness and demands of daily life, of finally getting back to meaningful activity. A friend gave me a book when she came to the Vineyard for Memorial Day weekend. On the first page there's a quote by Gloria Steinem. "Writing is the only thing that when I do it, I don't feel I should be doing something else."

It's the first Friday in June, sunny and beautiful. This morning I am crying in the car again. I miss the turn on the way to Woods Hole and almost miss the boat. Weekend trips to our summer home in Chilmark on the Vineyard are routine now.

There's no water at the house. The pump is broken. I feel overwhelmed. Can I hold my own with the repairman? Will I pay through the nose? I'm unprotected, making decisions alone.

Candy, a close friend, told me about another Chilmark woman, whose husband has "bad" cancer. He's going to die. Candy says Eleanor is very "strong." What does that mean? Eleanor says, "We're going to beat it." I remember saying and believing the same thing. Is that strength, or is it the only way to remain sane?

Strong. I think of what it is to be strong. I saw Dixie, my college friend, with her stalwart posture, sensible haircut, and runner's legs in tan shorts and a tee shirt pushing her twenty-four-year-old daughter's wheelchair down Trowbridge Street yesterday. Nan, shrunken, growing smaller, a scarf on her head, a padded white neck brace supporting her thin, still pretty face, holds a takeout lunch on her lap. They had been to Harvard Square bookstores in 90-degree heat. I stopped. Nan wanted to see our puppy. That's strong.

I try to mow the lawn. The lawn mower dies. I give up. I'll go get water and use my neighbor's bathroom instead of the woods. I'll be practical. Above all, Dixie is practical. Is that the source of her strength as she rolls her daughter, a Princeton graduate, with metastasized breast cancer, along the sidewalks of Cambridge?

Nan wanted to see the puppy but never did. The ebb and flow of her strength was so fragile yesterday that by the time I returned from my errands she was too weak to have visitors. Maybe tomorrow or next week, her mother said.

I wonder if I could ask Nan to say hello to Anatole when she dies. Tell him I'm all right, that I have a new puppy. Is he all right? Will Nan be all right? Will we, Dixie, Eleanor, and I be all right?

It seems that this all began, my husband's illness and his death, with our pump going out two years ago—to be precise, twenty-three months ago. Today, as I write the check to C. Kurth & Sons, who have just restored the water supply, I wonder if we were late in paying him the last time he was here, and is that why he wants $400 now and will bill the rest later. I wonder if I should explain to him that if we were late with that payment two years ago, it was because my husband had just been diagnosed with cancer. For eighteen years we had spent summers in this house and there were no problems with the well.

I have to go back to Cambridge this week to see a client. We've decided to bury Anatole on his birthday, July 16. I'll bring the ashes down when I come back on Wednesday.

I'm catching the bus to Woods Hole from the corner of Arlington and Columbus Streets in Boston at six-fifteen. I thought of calling a taxi because of the heaviness of the ashes and my tendency to tennis elbow, but instead I choose to walk. I had known this was coming. For the past eight months and three and a half weeks the ashes have been on top of the pine bureau in our bedroom in Cambridge. But today, finally, is the day for their journey to the Vineyard. At the end of this month the ashes, the soot, the charred bone fragments that are the earthly remains of my husband will be buried in Abel's Hill Cemetery in Chilmark under a maple tree.

I want to carry the ashes myself. I need to feel the strain on my elbow and back. I want to have memories that will include physical sensations. For this is the last physical thing that we will do together. I want there to be effort. I want there to be shortness of breath on this our last walk. I don't saunter or stroll. I walk with a purpose. I walk with the awareness and memories of our thirty years together. All the goodness and bad, all the pain and the pleasure are in this walk.

I walk faster than Anatole would have, for he was a *flâneur,* a stroller, a man of the boulevards, an observer. He needed time to savor. On our many walks, he commented on the world, and so did I, in a way that was part a sociological query, part gossip, and part amazement. But today I cannot linger. I am anxious about making the bus for Woods Hole, and if I slow down, I might be too flooded with feelings, and then I would collapse and cover the square box of ashes with my body and let out a widow's wail. There's a gravity inside me these days, a gravity that wants to pull me down and release all the anger, the tears, and the cries so they can blast the universe for what happened to my husband. So there I would have been on the Law School campus or in Harvard Yard wailing in a decibel range as high as any ghetto blaster but with none of the rhythm or tune, only the volume of despair.

My last walk with Anatole takes me past the Lesley College tennis court. He'd played so well there, hitting good ground strokes with Todd and Bliss. After weaving through the Lesley College buildings we get to the Law School campus. It is quiet and empty. I imagine Anatole commenting on the trees and lush foliage. I walk past a slim young girl wearing red-and-white running tights. I know Anatole would have looked her over. To be carrying his ashes and having this thought seems bizarre. The girl notices something in my face, and as we pass she gives me a look that I can only describe as consoling.

The ashes are in a Liberty vinyl bag that we'd bought in London a few years ago. Thank God there is no foresight, that the saleswoman hadn't said in a cheery, clipped English voice, "Yes, this a perfect bag to carry ashes in. It's deep enough and just the right shape."

Does it make sense that Anatole's last walk should be through Harvard Yard? He didn't even have a college degree. But he loved books, he loved literature. He had liked strolling though Harvard Yard. He liked looking at the students. Coming up from the Vineyard this morning I noticed that all of the grass on the Cape and outside of Boston is brown, bleached tan by the dryness of the summer. Here in Harvard Yard the large triangles of grass are bottle green matching the green paint of the dormitory doors. I wonder about the relation in life of water and illness and death. I wonder if it's water that is making this Harvard grass so green or is it the cross-fertilization of avid young minds. Then I notice the restored wooden hand pump to the side of the Yard. I'm tempted to see if I can get its water flowing.

I realize that it was prophetic that I'd run into David Kantor earlier. David our friend and therapist who helped us through some difficult emotions just before Anatole went into the hospital that last time. I hadn't seen him since the cremation service, and there he was today outside Evergood's, the neighborhood grocery store. He gave me a big bear hug. Whenever I see him I feel an infusion of energy. I need that now as the muscles begin to strain across my back. Carrying these ashes I need every muscle in my body to work. My legs, my back are strong from all the dance classes I've been taking. I won't injure myself on this last walk with Anatole.

We leave Harvard Yard, and I pause as we come within sight of Harvard Square. Across the street is the church in whose basement studio I dance. I look beyond the T entrance to the heart of the square, which is where the bookstores are. I wish there were time for one final browse at WordsWorth or Pangloss. But there is no time. So I go down into the T station. As I walk down the second set of stairs I think of how I hate full circles. Anatole and I once again underground. Years ago in the East Side Fourteenth Street stop on the IRT, I was stretching my calf on a step and Anatole followed me onto the train. And here we are again at the end of our last walk once more in a subway, underground, waiting together for a train. I stretch my calf on a step. A young woman looks at me with a puzzled expression. I need my ritual.

On the bus, my right leg presses against the box of ashes, which is wedged between my lower leg and the outside wall of the bus. We're passing over the Bourne Bridge, the only majestic moment on this trip. Anatole really should be carried upon a bier on a slow train through the countryside with crowds of readers gathered by the sides of the tracks. But no, this is right, this is private, the tiny space between my calf and the wall of the bus.

I'm always telling people I'm all right. Mostly they don't even ask. They just look. I jump the gun. I can't tolerate the waiting. I blurt out, "I'm all right." The need must be mine, to keep repeating to myself with others present that I'm all right. Why can't I say I'm terrible? The memories of Anatole's illness are like shards of glass in my stomach, in my spine, my soul. I shudder and lose my breath when I think of him curled up on a ferry seat trying not to throw up. When I think of his swollen feet—the fluids in his body losing direction, getting confused, flooding the dead ends of his once beautiful feet, distending the skin, the bones and structure of the feet that carried him through his life, these beautiful feet lost to his sight and mine.

Perhaps all I mean when I say I'm okay is that I'm alive, I'm upright. I'm not going to kill myself. I'm going to continue my life but it's going to be hard. It will require effort and concentration that I'm not sure I have. I'm not sure if I can do it. That's all I mean to say when I say I'm all right. I don't want people to worry about me. I want their help, but not their pity. That's no good to me. I know that it's not easy for them to stay with me, so however they do it I'm grateful. Anatole had the same complaints about friends when he was sick. He didn't want their pity. He wanted their radiance.

And he got that. There was radiance in the Dordogne a year ago May, among the six of us. Three couples, friends of many years, traveling together, we basked in one another's personalities, one another's quirks. We laughed and gamboled and teased and ate and ate. In my mind's eye I still see, as the four of us saw, as Ted, Candy, Jane, and I saw, as we peered down from the ruins high in the cliffs of La Roque Gagnac, we saw Anatole and Rick tossing a ball. In my mind's eye they are still there beneath the carefully patterned trees tossing the tennis ball that the French gardener found for them. Each man a graceful and stylish athlete discussing . . . what? Humanity, history, literature. They discuss these things as they continue to throw the ball back and forth with outstretched arms and flicking fingertips, shifting their weight from front to back, rocking with each throw.

I have to write these things, words bleeding the pain. Losing Anatole makes me sad and reflective and at the same time intense and wild. Simultaneously, I feel lost and capable, stranded and also moving at a furious pace as if I've been shot out of hell. I want some rest, some quiet. No, what I really want is to be met at the ferry by Anatole. I want to see him and his jaunty walk. He would be looking around, checking the scene.

Bliss meets me at the boat and we go to Sioux Eagle, our favorite jewelry store in Vineyard Haven. The ashes rest on the floor next to the display case as Bliss and I try on earrings. We both splurge. I buy the pair I'd seen on Memorial Day weekend, silver with jade drops. Bliss gets long silver feathers. Anatole would have protested and said we didn't need them. We already have enough earrings and we, each of us, certainly can't afford them. But there is a level of need. His death leaves us empty and frightened, and we need these brazen dangling earrings to face the world.

A few days later Bliss and her friend Jennifer are on the beach. They lie on the nude portion of Vincent Beach, flat on the sand, no bathing suits. Bliss keeps turning her head to the left looking back down the stretch of sand to Abel's Hill. This is a habit of summers past—to be on the lookout for her father, to see him before he sees her as he walks up the beach so she'll have time to put her suit back on. She maintains this measure of modesty between father and daughter. Only today she remembers with a start as she turns her head that he won't be walking down from Abel's Hill. At one point Bliss thinks she sees her father. There's a man with a similar walk.

Bliss and Jennifer talk about what it means for Anatole not to be here. Bliss says, "Well, my life isn't so different today from when he died nine months ago, so there's not a whole lot that I want him to know, but what about ten years from now when I'm established in my work, when I'm married and have children. I want him to know about those things and he won't." Bliss and Jennifer cry as they think about Bliss getting married without her father. Who will walk her down the aisle?

Jennifer tells me all this later, after she's taken Bliss to the boat.

This is the first time that I'm traveling down to Woods Hole without crying. It's a beautiful summer day and I feel pleasure in returning to Chilmark and Abel's Hill, with its familiar trees and smells and gorgeous beach. Then I take out my notebook and read about walking with the ashes, and my mood darkens. I think about how pleasure and happiness and crying and sorrow can exist together, on the same day, in the same person. How do I live with or balance these two emotions? What is their relation to each other? How can they happen at the same time? Both feelings have their reality. If there were only sorrow I might break. If there were only pleasure, I would be crazy. The thing is to stay with both.

Leaving the boat today I see an old man getting into a wheelchair. Another man flips down one of the footrests. The old man's face rises. The eyeballs slowly look up. The rest of the expression is missing, the smile, the configuration of thanks or of recognition. There is nothing, only the slow rising of the focus. Anatole did that in those last days in the hospital, as if the movement of his eyes took all the energy that was available. Where were the thoughts behind those eyes? Where was his mind, his reaction, his response? What was it like for Anatole to have lost his split-second timing? How could he stand it? What became of his impatience?

It's hot in the house today. Late in the morning Candy, who has a pottery studio here in Chilmark, comes over with two urns that she has made, one large, one small. The larger one is glazed white and decorated with the tools of Anatole's craft. A yellow legal pad, pencils, books, eyeglasses. Candy and I transfer Anatole's ashes to the urn at 11:55 a.m. I save some for myself and put them with my hands in the small white jar sprigged with yellow and lavender flowers. We seal both with Duco Cement glue. There are still some ashes left. Perhaps we'll distribute them among friends, perhaps the beach. I will have to ask Todd and Bliss. This Saturday friends will gather in the Abel's Hill Cemetery and Candy's urn will be buried. The Reverend Wallace, a neighbor, will say a few words. I've decided to read what I wrote about my last walk with Anatole, the journey of his ashes from Cambridge to here.

Since noon, since Candy left, there has been a horizontal plane of emptiness reaching out from me in all directions. I wander through this hot house. I look at the epilogue that I need to send off. I search for an eraser to correct typos. Slowly I go downstairs. I have forgotten what I'm looking for. I feed the dogs and come back upstairs and then remember the eraser. I again go downstairs and wonder about putting a sweatshirt in the washer. Candy had put Dawn dishwashing fluid on the grass smudges—her cure for stubborn stains. I have no confidence in my ability to remove stains. I failed with the cancer. Are stains the stigmata of the vulnerable? To be marked, does that mean one will die?

I'm awash with the emptiness, the quietness. I can't function. No, that's not true. I can and I will. I'll sweep the floor. Anatole's words, his ashes, they will all find their place.

It's been twenty-three months now since the diagnosis and nine months since Anatole died. I continue to go on. Back in Cambridge as I walk to dance class I begin to think about myself. I realize I am finding my body again, and this helps. I had really lost it these past two years.

Years ago I trained as a dancer at the Juilliard School and later with Martha Graham in New York and Mary Wigman in Germany. Anatole had taken the subway uptown to Harlem dance halls, learning the moves and rhythms of Tito Puente, Mongo Santamaria, and other greats of Afro-Cuban music. He could also do a mean lindy. When rock dancing came along he invented his own style of strutting leg flourishes, hip twists, and arm flings. In the sixties and seventies we'd go to Aux Puces and Nepenthe in New York, small, chic dance clubs. In the summer our favorite place to dance was the Seaview in Oak Bluffs on the Vineyard, a run-down hotel across the street from the water. Local groups, Kitch'n Sync, Taylor Made, Johnny and the Bluefish, played loud, stompy music through sweaty crowded nights—a dancing free-for-all with breaks on the side porch. We would go with friends and dance in groups. Later as our kids got older they would come too. The night before our son left for college we went dancing. I cried all the way to the Seaview in the car, overwhelmed by the sadness of his childhood ending now that he was leaving home. There was a particularly good band that night, and later I thought about how we are a family who can dance our way through tough times.

While the children were growing up I taught modern dance and performed on and off with dance companies in Connecticut, where we lived for twenty-five years. When I switched careers and began social work in 1982, I had to cut back to an

occasional dance class and I relied on sporadic running to keep
my body intact. With the move to Cambridge and Anatole's illness I exercised even less.

About a year ago I saw a flyer for Marcus Schulkind's classes
in Boston and Cambridge. He is a dancer and choreographer
from New York whom I'd known back in the early seventies. I
checked again on his schedule and learned that he was teaching
three days a week in a church basement in Harvard Square. I
struggled through a class. He didn't recognize me. At the end of
class I reintroduced myself. He is a gifted teacher and I've begun
to take his class with regularity.

Dancing is leading me back to life, to my strengths. It's hard
and sometimes frightening, learning new moves, new combinations, twists, turns, sudden falls, quick steps, and changes of
direction. The phrases are too long. There's too much detail in
them. I want simpler, more symmetrical patterns. I want to
move as a pair, have a partner to cross the long diagonal space
in the studio, be in sync with breath and gesture and energy.
Instead I struggle with the center-floor combinations, where
you're on your own if you really want to dance.

In class, if I keep following along, eventually I catch on to
pieces of the combination, certainly not the whole phrase. I
don't get the rhythmic patterns clearly or the dynamics, only the
larger shapes. All the while I feel awkward, slightly slow and stupid. I'm bored by having to pay attention in order to catch on.
Eventually, when I begin to get the phrase, something else clicks
in. I experience the sense of asserting myself. When I'm really
sure of the phrase I can dare to take some chances and put more
of myself into it. Then it feels wonderful, and I realize that these
long phrases are a way in which I can explore who I am and
expand the repertoire of how I move.

Howard Moss, a poet friend, sent me Mozart piano tapes
when Anatole was in the hospital. I played them over and over as
I drove back and forth to the hospital each day. At a time when I
had no body, the music reminded me of ballet class, of muscles

working. After Anatole died I couldn't play them for a long time. I couldn't play them until I started dancing again.

Sitting in the bath tonight, I remembered my doubts as a child that I could float or stay buoyant in the water. I knew that water gave some support, but I also knew that there had to be some type of treading movement to keep afloat. And even though I might have been able to manage that for a brief spell, I knew that the sinking would eventually take over. Maybe that's why it was so vitally important for me to learn to dance. I have always needed to know the right moves.

In class today Marcus said these things:

Regarding attachments as from muscle to muscle. Don't grip. Instead pull up and through.

If you have a special gift, you have to work that much harder to use it. A gift means more work, not less.

His comment to me. Be sure to use your history. Don't ignore your history, your muscle memory. Marcus reminded me that I know a lot. I have a rich source of patterns and shapes, so I should retrieve them.

In walking down to Harvard Square I remembered the emphasis at Yale Psychiatric Institute, where I worked in New Haven, in articulating the separation, the loss. How did that help the patients? Supposedly it kept them from regressing. I am working on articulating my body, and it seems to keep me from falling apart.

Marcus also told me that when I get tired or exhausted, don't grab. Instead breathe and reach down and find another way.

Brook

My brother died today, July 26, on our son's birthday. Brook sixty and Todd twenty-seven. The call came at 6:15 p.m. A summer storm blew in with thunder and lightning. Now at 11:30 a steady rain with its soothing tempo is falling on the uninsulated pine roof. I undress for bed, finally alone, tears welling. Dinner with the friends who hugged and fed me tonight was normal in some respects. I think of the time in Norway after my mother died. Those difficult two days before I could fly home were filled with ordinary activities, shopping in Oslo and on Sunday a visit to a seaside cabin, swimming in the icy water, the intensity of the cold, its sensation, a memory to have forever, the chill of the water easier to remember than the event it shields. If she were still alive, not killed in the car accident north of Oslo in June of 1957, if she were alive, the pain of her son dying would be overwhelming. My mother's face would break apart.

About to crawl into my own bed, I see my brother, now cold and lifeless, lying on a pallet in a mortuary. Where was he when he collapsed? Was he standing or sitting? What was the position of his arms and legs? Did he fall or slump? What was he wearing? What were his thoughts just before his heart exploded? What kind of day had he had?

My house here is being rented for August. I'll have to finish pulling it together tomorrow. Then I can leave for Vermont.

Making the turn onto Route 11, going down into Manchester, I am dropping into emptiness, feeling the loss of Brook as I descend into the valley, the empty valley where he no longer lives. The road keeps going down and down. There is no bottom to my stomach. I drift down, no parachute needed to slow this leisurely free fall, the fall into the place where I no longer have a brother.

Barbara, my sister, has flown up from Florida. Together we will finish the final chapter of our brother's life. There is a house filled with treasures and junk, each object sacred to my brother's heart. He collected old toys, marine antiques, guns, cars, old motors, washing machines, lawn mowers, parts for engines. A few blocks away there is his car dealership, a business to be either shut down or sold, but a business that has to be kept going in the interim. We don't know where to begin with all of this.

Days are filled with lawyers, papers, arrangements for a memorial service, anxious employees at the car dealership. We learn from our lawyer that Margaret, my brother's live-in girlfriend, is upset because there was no will, and she is angered by being left with nothing. They had been together for three years, but my brother was not happy with her. He would call me in Cambridge on Saturday mornings from his dealership searching for a way to end the relationship. And yet he couldn't. He wanted her out of his life and he also needed her.

Barbara and I have been concerned about her situation and

want to help her, as she has been a part of our brother's life. She does have means of her own and grown children. We let her know that she can live in Brook's home until she had the emotional energy to go on with her life. We share a common grief. Barbara and I stay at a local hotel.

With my brother's estate, his house, and his business, at every juncture we are pressed by those in the community with vested interests in getting a piece of the action or controlling the disposition of assets. Barbara and I are referred to as "the sisters," flat-landers invading the inner sanctum of how this town deals with its own.

There is a place that one can get to which is beyond the ken of ordinary life. Normal priorities and concerns disappear. It is not possible to pay attention to world news because of what is happening at the tip of one's nose—as when a husband is dying or a brother dies and leaves so much unsettled business. Today there has been a major coup in Russia and a hurricane along the northeast coast. I don't know how to register the news of these events because my curiosity has been drained of its ability to be interested in anything at all. All I knew this evening was that I needed shampoo for my hair.

I've always thought that curiosity was an indicator of a person's mental health. The only thing in my life that I know or think about now is the problems related to my brother's death.

Even with all the demands of the current drama, there are times that I withdraw, not an ordinary withdrawal, but a pulling back, pulling in to that place where I am with the memories of one year ago, last August. Those days when each hour, each minute was measured and ruled by the work and effort of Anatole swallowing the pills that I believed would save him. I would badger him, watch him, my eyes as hungry as his for a way to undo his illness. Restore us to health. Restore my husband to health. Please God, he can't die.

Most of the time it was watching the clock and shopping for and preparing the special foods that Anatole usually couldn't get down. There was a feeling of triumph if he did get one meal down. I was sure that the organic foods, specially prepared, would save him, would build up good cells that would over-power the bad cells that were slowly ravaging his body, the body that had lain next to mine, made babies with mine, tossed and hugged and intertwined with mine for twenty-nine years, the smooth skin, the strong, sinewy muscles, the flat belly, the slen-der hips. How did that rottenness begin? Why did it rage?

Actually I never asked why. I accepted it all, except I didn't believe that Anatole could die. Did *he*? Did he believe, did Ana-tole know that he was going to die. I was an idiot. I was blind. I refused to see. I could only see the fact that he still had arms, that he still had eyes, a voice, a nose. These familiar parts of my hus-band blinded me to the rumblings, the storming of the cancer cells in his prostate.

But then how could I know the intensity of pain he was feel-ing? He tried so desperately to be graceful about it. At times he would lose the ability to be ironic. The swagger would leave, and then he would become short-tempered and accuse me of annoy-ing him with meals and ministrations. His pain eluded me. It was hidden. I couldn't see or touch or smell or hear his pain. It was encased in his body. The pain tricked me. It disguised and enrobed itself with the familiar features and contours of my hus-band. By my not recognizing the pain, it overpowered me, it overpowered us. It drained us both of our good tempers until we only had the grit and grime of worn-out emotions.

Woke up at 5 a.m. and couldn't get back to sleep. Even with these busy frenetic days in Manchester, moving from crisis to crisis, the events of a year ago keep breaking through. The only blessing of all this furor and sadness in Vermont is that I don't dwell on last August and memories of Anatole's illness all the time. What would it have been like if I'd been at the Vineyard? Would I have been too much of a drain on friends? Should these things be talked about—the vomiting, the nausea, the sudden crash of a fall, the enduring and the not enduring of pain.

All these memories were at the edge of my consciousness this morning, there to be seen and re-remembered if only I would turn my head. I realize I don't know how to live with them. I can imagine a photo album of these memories. Anatole on the bathroom floor after he'd fallen, Anatole curled up in bed in a tight snail-like position with no hard shell to protect him from the pain, Anatole leaning over the rail of our deck retching up the half cup of cereal he'd managed to get down, Anatole swallowing the sixth of the eight pills he had to take six times daily, the expression of concentration and defeat on his face, Anatole in the small wing chair, the one with the dark floral fabric, talking animatedly with his new babysitter from the Cambridge hospice, high on Ritalin, not looking sick but having just thirty minutes earlier hemorrhaged blood from his penis, large clots in the toilet that we both saw. How did he endure all this? How did I? How did we manage?

We were very much alone last August, the two of us in our Cambridge house. One day I went out and bought three bookcases for my study and painted them off-white.

From August 13 to 28 there was a desperate attempt to get onto the Gonzalez program, with the 160 pills per day and organic foods. It was like being in the middle of the Atlantic Ocean in a storm trying to climb onto a life raft that wouldn't hold. The flotation devices kept sinking beneath us. They were too slippery to hold on to. Waves would crash over us and push us back down into the dark water.

If I could capture these images and arrange them in an album, who would one day sit and look at them? Would it be me, Todd, Bliss, our friends, the grandchildren that Anatole will never know? Is there knowledge or a hidden epiphany in these scenes? Is there an "aha" experience here? Oh, so that's what dying, what cancer is like. One doesn't realize all the choreography, all the gestures and postures that are part of illness, all the contortions of body and face. Well, it is part of living, this dying business.

I sit here by the side of the pulled-back drape of the motel window in the early, pale, overcast light, not wanting to turn on a lamp for fear of waking my sister, who is sleeping twenty feet away from me. I look across a stretch of lawn. There is a grove of trees beyond. I study the branches near the top, which are being rustled by a small breeze. I think of all the moments in my life when I have looked out of windows and gazed at branches, moments of being alone and still.

One Year Later

Today is September 10, the day that Anatole's bladder burst. What happened last September, is it any less shocking because it occurred a year ago? Time for me is shifting, deflating, losing its ability to measure. If I could collapse time entirely, life and death would lose their meaning. Existence would be all the time or none of the time, and pain would be all of the time or not at all.

These words, which make no sense, keep me away from Anatole. I want him here in the room with me reading a book and sipping a beer.

The pencil I pick up has a sharp point. I wonder if Anatole sharpened it. He always kept a ready supply of sharpened pencils on his desk. One day there will be only one pencil left in the house that Anatole sharpened. I wonder if this is it.

Did Anatole's bladder burst or did it just disintegrate? The memories have been coming to me throughout the day. I was lifting him up. What were we trying to do? I was supporting his back and lifting when Mona, the nurse, shouted "Code!" and pushed me out of the room.

There was the conversation with Dr. Kantoff. My silent howl. The scream that stayed inside me. The scream that's still there. I screamed when my mother died. I had been driving the car. But no screams now. Not once in this past year has my breath forced through my throat and mouth a cry that would give voice to my pain, voice to Anatole's pain. Only these words. These words that are ciphers of the caverning of pain that exists inside and around me, pain that is trying to match the physical pain that Anatole endured.

When there was an hour, an afternoon, an evening when the pain was particularly bad, Anatole would retreat to bed to lie on his side pulled into himself. A psychic once told me that I had healing hands, nonsense to me at the time, but when the cancer was piercing I would curl myself behind my husband and gently massage his ribs and spine to ease what he described as the rat-gnawing pain eating into his bones. He said this touching helped. When his breathing was easier, I would stay in bed and read out loud, *Brideshead Revisited.* He believed that words used well, a story unfolding, would ease the pain. He chose *Brideshead,* a book about love and longing and, finally, about dying, religion, and God and the need for the red light of an altar to continue to burn—for a belief, a knowledge that can't be told in words or thought or contained in human emotion—for this knowledge to continue to burn.

Is the pain of Anatole's illness the red flame that burns within me, that sears the marrow of my bones? Is this pain, this red flame, some kind of knowledge of God that has been bequeathed to me? Is this my gift? Is this how Anatole's death has changed me? Never to be the same again, always to have the red flame, the pain scorching my breath, intensifying my need for water, to be near water, on water. Perhaps this red light will illuminate the world for me. Tonight when Bliss came home she said I could cry with her, but I turned away, saying I wanted to be alone.

· · ·

Last week I went to a wedding in Connecticut. The daughter of some close friends was married on her parents' lawn. It was good to see former neighbors. One of the guests began talking about a wellness program that he was inaugurating at the winter resort Snowbird, in Utah. There was to be a trial run beginning later that week to be attended by invited guests. He wondered if I'd like to come along. I said yes.

Getting on the plane today, I sense the presence and at the same time the lack of presence of Anatole. Boarding a plane is something we've done together these past thirty years. This is the first plane I've been on since he died.

I walk down the aisle and look for my seat. I have two large carry-on bags. There's a sudden pang as I realize that there is no one behind me to place my luggage in the overhead rack. As I struggle to lift the heavier one up into the tight space, an arm reaches over my shoulder to help. I don't turn my head or say thank you.

We always traveled coach and I would have the window seat, Anatole the middle. We would sit shoulder to shoulder. I would hold his hand tightly during takeoff. He was a buffer between myself and the other passengers. In turn I would soothe his impatience if there was a delay. Loosening his belt and pulling out his glasses, large square horn-rimmed glasses that would sit low on his nose, he'd begin to read the book he'd brought along. I would look out the window, read the airplane magazine, and jabber about concerns at home or details of our trip.

After the meal, as the cabin lights darkened for the movie, I would curl up in my seat, the armrest raised and a blanket over me. Anatole would have carefully tucked me in and then I'd sleep, leaning my weight against his shoulder and side. Through the night he would alternate between reading and watching the movie. He never used a headset to hear the sound. He claimed he could provide a better story to accompany the images than the screenwriter. He did not sleep. Was that because his life was a vigil? Is that what a writer does even at 35,000 feet above the Atlantic in the middle of the night?

The seat belt sign turns off and stewardesses begin to roam the aisle offering magazines and refreshments. I feel the exhaustion of too many nights of meager sleep, five or six hours at the most in the past week. I move back to the empty part of the plane and have three seats to myself. I could easily lift the armrests out of the way and lie down and sleep for a few hours, but now I have the task of vigilance. To look, to observe, to comment, to continue to try to figure out the twists and turns of this world, its conformation, flavor, joy, pain. Last night while walking to a theater in Harvard Square my friend Sherry quoted a seventeenth-century haiku master. "Every day is a journey and the journey is home."

A few hours later, somewhere over the Midwest, the land is flat, patterned squares of green interspersed with beige. The tan areas have shadowed flumes in them. The earthy patches mimic marble from this height. Down there, 30,000 feet below, the earth, the middle of the United States, looks like a kitchen floor.

Fifteen minutes later foothills begin, dark, ominous, erratic shapes disrupting the orderly geometry of the rectilinear plains. Their darkness insinuates and creeps with shadowy, curving forms acknowledging the force that pushed them up from below. Suddenly there is a perfectly round lake with a smaller lake next to it. Two meteors, siblings, had landed side by side.

Then a small strand of mountains, their rock faces reflecting sun, and a high meadow of green where one could be alone and wise. On the far side of this range there is a city with a racecourse and an airfield. Canyons beyond. All the land is brown, the strong, warm shades of fall clothing, with rippling, corrugated hills and the dried-up squiggles of riverbeds.

. . .

A week of seminars, hikes, new faces, conviviality, exercise classes, a rope course, all fine-tuned to promote wellness and better living, all these things turn my face toward the sun and the beauty of distant views. About forty of us, guinea pigs mostly from Texas, Utah, and California, are staying at the main hotel in Snowbird, a large copper stone edifice, a twin of the Seagram Building in New York City, which having wandered west stumbled into this high valley and lay down on its side. On the roof of the hotel there is a heated pool. At seven each morning I go up and float on my back and watch rays of sun slowly turn the red canyon walls that bracket the valley to bronze. I am the only person there, passive and buoyant in the water. These are the moments that I treasure the most, these mornings and the final hike.

The last day here Dick Bass, who is hosting the week, leads us on a trek across the mountains to a series of his favorite views. At rest stops he tells us how he'd reached the top of Mt. Everest at age fifty with only two prior weeks of fitness training. He'd kept slogging ahead, right leg, left leg. When he had no energy and could barely breathe at 17,000 feet, he'd make himself laugh at jokes he'd repeat out loud and then he would recite poetry. As a child in Texas, he and his father would take long drives and memorize poems as a way of countering the monotony of the endless straight roads. Kipling was their favorite. Words, again, pulling one forward and through.

Back in Cambridge, away from the high mountain sun and air, grief returns, slow-moving, viscous waves. I feel a greater pull in gravity. I'm heavier. Everything is heavier. There's a recurring soreness in my throat as if I'd spent hours screaming.

The difficulty of this time is that I, on some level, am waiting, just waiting. It's as if I'm in a distant terminal, say a bus station in Omaha, sitting, standing, and walking back and forth between the newsstand and a candy machine, unable to make any decisions about what to read or what to do.

I am stuck in this house, the house that Anatole and I found ourselves in the day he was diagnosed. Both of us had a history of dreaming that we had bought and moved into a house that was depressing, ill-suited. That bad dream had come true, except it was not only the wrong house, Anatole's body had become the wrong body. His body, which had aged so little, betrayed him, and now I'm sitting, waiting. Am I waiting for my body to betray me? Can I will that? Is the grief I'm feeling now, the boundless grief that has no edges, no pauses, is this sadness the pull toward Anatole? Is it that I cannot be separated from him and so I need to crumble and decay and rot internally, that I need to find my own cancer, cause my own cells to be aberrant, wild, untamed so that these cells can be once again wedded, once again committed to my husband?

Looking at the two black dogs in our back yard, George Eliot and Player, I recall how our family has always had its pairs, two children, two dogs, two cats, and then the pair of husband and wife, father and mother. Now the balance is upset. As in an amputation, the phantom other half lingers and is at the same time absent and present. This contradiction of being here and not being here is unsettling.

Grieving, this is the point, not the loss. The loss is a fact, a happening. The grief, the feeling is the experience, the resonance, the residue. It's what interferes with functioning. It distracts. It also draws one to oneself, one's center and the currents there, the emptiness, the fear. What is the task? To express grief. To make it conscious. To go through it. To stay with it, not to avoid. To be alive to it. By being alive to my grief I'm alive to my life.

The day before Thanksgiving, I'm alone in the car, quiet, with two sleeping dogs and two sleeping cats, animals breathing in tune with the hum of the ship's diesel motor. The scene at Woods Hole is like a Norman Rockwell painting, families coming and going, brightly colored clothes, parcels of food, duffel bags, dogs straining at their leashes, each person part of a group with a destination, a place to go.

My place feels shaky. Where is my home? Who are my relatives? Without Anatole the immediate family—Todd, Bliss, and myself—is fractured. There are awkward spaces between us. We've begun to see a family therapist. Last night's session was raw with tears and strong feelings. We are reaching for one another but we're too far apart to touch. They are coming down tomorrow morning. They both had plans tonight in Cambridge. We'll have Thanksgiving dinner with Suzy and Hugh and their family and a day of beach walks on Friday. Saturday morning they will go back to their lives.

Sunday night. Five days on the Vineyard. I'm leaving tomorrow at 5 p.m. I haven't done any of the work I brought down. I planted forty bulbs and moved a few plants and learned to tend the new woodstove, but that's it. I spent some time with friends and knit and read a bit of Wittgenstein's biography. A mild cold saps me of energy and motivation.

Ray Monk, writing about Wittgenstein, says that for him and others of his generation, as they went off to fight in World War One, their response to possible death was the gain of the spiritual value it would bring. What Wittgenstein wanted from the war was a transformation of his whole personality—"a variety of religious experience that would change his life irrevocably."

Before leaving for the ferry I go out to the side yard and adjust the cover on *Swallow.* It had been improperly supported this past year because I couldn't find the beam support, so the canvas had sagged in one spot and became filled with dirty water and leaves. I take the cover partially off to clear away the debris and that's when I see the boat's registration number with its date of '88. This was the last time *Swallow* was in the water, the summer of 1988. Since then she's been neglected, sitting in Connecticut for a year, exposed to the elements with no cover, and now in the Vineyard on our lawn for two years. As I sweep off the twigs and broken acorns brought on board by squirrels, I notice the grime and stains that cover the topside of what was once a trim, clean, pale blue–and–white boat. Now there are large brown amoeba-shaped discolorations and flaking paint. It's as if Anatole's cancer with its decay and rot had been at work on this sturdy boat. She seems fragile to me today, this 2,800-pound fiberglass replica of the original wooden catboats of the turn of the last century. Can she be saved? Can I restore her? Is her condition also the condition of my life? Can I be saved? Can I be restored?

Anatole couldn't be saved even with all my efforts. I was so convinced that he would outlive the cancer that when he lost his battle, part of me was lost. The first year after Anatole died I kept going out of habit and out of fear. I woke up each morning and continued to breathe and eat. I even took dance classes and began to feel good with my body. Now twelve months have passed and I sense I'm different. There's a way in which I don't care about myself or what happens to me. I am detached from things that should concern me. I have been abandoned by myself just as I abandoned *Swallow*, and like *Swallow* my canvas cover has rotted because I don't care enough to make the adjustments, to keep my life taut and trim, so there is debris, discoloration, and flaking paint everywhere I look. If I didn't have to work in Cambridge to support myself I would come down to the Vineyard and just do maintenance work. Scrape, paint, restore, renew.

Tonight my cold continues. Standing at the kitchen sink I can hear Anatole saying, "You should get some rest. Go to bed. Your cold won't get better if you don't rest. Leave that."

He continues to take care of me. In some strange way I don't feel that he is gone. He will always be with me as the one who really cares. Cared. What verb tense do I use? It's confusing.

Also, if Anatole continues to be with me, will I ever be able to let anyone else in?

Walking from the post office to Wordsworth this afternoon I realized that there are few streets in Cambridge and few book-shops that I did not wander through with Anatole. In the brief months of his illness and of our lives here, he and I walked up and down and across and around. I know what he would be looking at in a store window, know where he would be in a bookstore, in the fiction or travel section, sometimes biography. I don't remember our specific conversations while walking, but I do have a sense of their alertness, the quality of observation. We were always looking and noticing a scene, a detail, an architec-tural eccentricity, a cozy corner, a non sequitur.

I have been told today that my cat, my little five-pound, feisty feline, Jassy, has a large tumor pressing on her windpipe. It's inoperable. Here I am again watching a cancer pressing on and invading a basic bodily function of someone I love. She just ate some scallops and now she has to open her mouth and suck in each breath.

Bliss comes in and silently rubs my shoulder. I decide to sleep downstairs on the love seat next to Jassy, who's on the end table snuggled into an improvised bed of towels and pillows. I close my eyes and notice the regularity of my breathing. It's possible that she might die in the night. When I stayed with Anatole at Dana Farber I would try to match my breathing to his so that he could sync in with it when his breath was labored. It had always been important to him for us to run in the same rhythm, so I knew he would respond to my breath and in this way I could get him through the night.

In the morning I take Jassy to the vet. The first shot misses the vein and she howls in pain. The second shot puts her "to sleep."

.   .   .

A late-December Saturday, not cold, quite temperate and sunny, but I wake up as I went to bed, with heaviness and loneliness. Sherry calls, but I won't talk. I hang up. Bliss asks me if I'm going to take ballet class with her. All I can say is, I don't know. Then ten minutes later I come downstairs and say let's go.

Walking into the dance studio Bliss talks about the good snow for skiing up north and suggests that she, Todd, and I go. I reply flatly that I can't think of taking a day off until my obligations are under control. I sense as I'm saying this the sourness in my voice. Bliss says then perhaps she and Todd can go.

As we climb the stairs up to the studio (Marcus is now above ground), I'm aware I'm being the martyr: not a martyr with purpose as in Martha Graham's *Seraphic Dialogue*—but rather a martyr who only repeats a litany of complaints. I also know that the work of the class, the effort involved, will shift my mood. Move a muscle, change a thought. Simplistic axioms used to annoy Anatole. He didn't like flat rhetoric. And in its way, it's the flatness of a depression that I feel—more than feel, for I have become flat, flat and dull-witted, repetitive, uncommunicative, pasty-faced. The blood congeals in my veins to make a sloweddown, dull-eyed person.

In the class I begin to push and stretch. I'm very out of shape. I feel motivated to get to daily classes. I wonder if I can afford the cost and time, but then can I afford the flatness, the deadness?

After class Bliss and I stop at Savenors to pick up a chicken for lunch. James Atlas and his son are coming over, and I'm going to make chicken soup because they've both had colds.

There is no choosing when one dies. Anatole didn't want to die. He wanted to live. He wanted to finish his book on Greenwich Village. He wanted to write his book on talk, but instead his ureters blocked. He had no choice. He was not consulted as to the timetable for all this carnage. He had choice in his attitude and reactions but no choice in the event itself. He would choose to be alive today, to have been here today at the dining room table with Jim and his son William, to coax William into letting himself be held by a strange man, to exchange literary opinions and prejudices with Jim. His choice today would have been to walk around Fresh Pond with the pups. Player would have exasperated him.

Why is it that we don't have choice about some things in our lives? What does it mean that good and bad just happen to us? Is there a lesson? Does it mean we just have to accept? All these words are empty and useless in the presence of a killing cancer.

Jassy's windpipe began to close off on December 15 because of a cancerous tumor. Did I accept that? No, I despaired. I cried. I felt alone and lost and betrayed. All I can trust in is life, and yet when life is snuffed out, taken away, that in which I trust is also stolen, and what stays is desolation.

I am confused. Is it just emptiness at the end and the absence of life, or is there transcendence? Perhaps the only transcendence we have is hearing music, seeing a sunset, being at rest in the arms of a loved one—special moments of life

I am despairing and alone and yet I have no hesitation about going on. I don't mind feeling terrible. Is this acceptance? I know, however, that I prefer happiness.

It is almost the New Year, and I'm at my desk, hearing a few faint pops, single firecrackers. I imagine that I hear the fireworks over Boston Harbor, but they are too far away.

It has been a hard day. I picked up Jassy's ashes at five-thirty. Then I came home and curled up on my bed, cradling her ashes between chest and knees. I yearned for her impetuousness, her inability to be still, her need to have it her way, the annoyance of having her around. She could fill a room and a house with her presence.

I lay on my bed and cried, Jassy's ashes against my stomach, Brook's ashes under the bed, and some of Anatole's ashes on the bureau. Outside the shuttered windows the fireworks with a muffled noise sounded like popcorn popping.

Then I ate some dinner and tried to watch television but gave up after a while. So I went to my desk and for almost three hours wrote five and a half pages about why I can't sit at my desk.

Writing is the best way to be with myself. Words pulling one forward and through.

Why I Can't Sit at My Desk

On top of my writing pad, lying on the blue blotter, there are layers of bills, receipts, grocery slips, parking tickets, letters from banks with meaningless instructions. They are all shuffled together. Sometimes Belle, our Vineyard coon cat, sleeps on the desk, so papers have fallen on the floor. Just beyond the blotter there is a northeast-facing window that receives morning sun, a patch of warmth the cat has found. When she wakes, she stretches and scratches herself. Cat hair and cat dander shift down through her nest.

Sometimes I try to sort through these papers. I make piles and toss, but within a week, like the debris left by the tide after a storm, there are new envelopes, half-opened announcements, and more instructions from banks. Since Anatole's and Brook's deaths there has been an onslaught of paper. Medical bills, insurance forms, bank forms, transfers of property, inventories of property, probate forms, affidavits, current bills, past-due bills.

As I attempt to sort through these papers I always come upon
something that destroys my composure. From day to day I try to
give the impression—and usually succeed—of being functional
and a survivor, but I'm not. The façade is a sham. I am thrashing
around and waiting to drown. Today it was the Visa slip for the
repair insurance on Todd's secondhand car. We had paid $495
so he would be protected from car repair bills. This was on January 19, 1989, not quite two years ago. When the car later that
spring needed repairs, we just paid up front. We didn't have time
to figure out the insurance. Actually we probably forgot that we
had it.

This forgetting, this not paying attention to the details of life
when a family member is sick means that there are other losses.
It's as if one's whole life is a boat that has sprung a series of small
but persistent leaks. Credits that don't get redeemed, bills paid
twice, stains on carpets that don't get blotted out, clothes left at
the dry cleaners for so long that they disappear. When we went
to England for a week in February, while Anatole was still well
enough to travel, there was a mix-up on tickets and we had to
purchase an extra one at the airport for $900. We were never
reimbursed. In my head I can add up $5,000 of misplaced and
unclaimed money.

When I sit at my desk and see a piece of paper that reminds
me that there was no time, no space, no way to figure out how to
get the refund or send in the forms for the reimbursement, I
once again know that strain and the hopelessness. As I am now I
was then. I kept the façade of optimism, but I was often desperate and wild with fear.

This is why I can't sit at my desk, because invariably there is a
scrap of paper that pulls me back to the place from which I
watched my husband die.

To watch someone die is a terrible experience. It fills one with
dread, and after the person dies, the dread remains. It carves out
a space inside of you and settles in for the long haul. The dread
saps your energy, leaves you inert. The definition of *inert* from

my grandfather's 1942 Funk & Wagnalls dictionary is "destitute of inherent power to move." That's what the dread has done to me. Any project, no matter how small, is overwhelming.

For months now I find that I have great trouble going to the post office. There are usually two trips involved, because I almost always forget either an address or part of the item to be mailed. Everything in my life is apparently an emergency and so needs to be Express Mailed or at the very least Priority Mailed, and so the mailing envelopes get addressed at the post office. With this simple exercise of floundering at the post office and then returning home to get the missing piece I prove to myself over and over again that I am lame, out of focus, disorganized, and stumbling.

It's as if the wildness, the anger, the horror at my husband's illness and my brother's sudden untimely death, having no way to get out, these feelings short-circuited some internal wiring, ripping out cords and connections inside of me. No one sees these internal scars, but I can sense them and I know that this internal wreckage hobbles me.

Shortly after we moved to Wendell Street in August of 1989, I noticed a Chinese man attempting to run back and forth on the sidewalk at the other end of the block. He was spastic and ran with a jerky motion. With every fourth or fifth step a sudden contraction of his left side would cause him to trip and almost fall, but he would catch his balance and run another four steps before this would happen again.

Recently I saw a similar-looking man running up Mass Ave., near the Arlington line, about two miles away, with an almost normal stride. I'm not sure it's the same person. I'd like to believe that it is.

I suppose I could see this man's progress as a lesson to learn from, but I'm obstinate. I quarrel that I'm not Chinese. I don't have a singularity of purpose. The man is probably obsessed with biomolecular research, and so he has the training of being intently focused. But that is not my makeup. Mine is the sprawl and the clutter and the drip, drip of the leaky faucet and the chill breeze of the uninsulated floor. It's insurance claims that don't get mailed, the lost parking ticket whose fine gets doubled because it wasn't paid on time. This is how I externalize my dread, the dread that is the loss.

Last year, during the Gulf War, there were pictures on CNN of houses in Israel that had been hit by Scud missiles. Walls were torn away, but there was still furniture in the rooms. The suction of the force, the gust that pulled the walls away, left small objects and papers jumbled and piled in odd corners. This is familiar. This is what my study and my kitchen table look like. I'm not able to sort through it. I can't seem to restore order. At least not yet.

A Life Alone

What does it mean, a life alone? How do I conceive of a life without my husband? In a way he continues to be with me. His standards, his prejudices remain with me. An intolerance of boredom, a need for stylish clothes, for a taut, athletic body, a desire for lively, intelligent companions, a love of grace and artfulness, all these things were important to Anatole as they are now to me.

Without my husband I discover that I'm more of a me. People tell me I look wonderful. I know, I sense, I feel that. Work has expanded. Besides my private psychotherapy practice, I'm seeing clients two and a half days a week in two mental health clinics, one in Andover and the other at New England Memorial Hospital in Stoneham. And there is my dancing.

I'm on a schedule of four to five dance classes a week at the Green Street Studio in Central Square, where Marcus now teaches. As I drive there each morning I think about what it is to dance. In class you practice and develop muscles that work together with sustained effort to hold your bones, your self, your blood, organs, and tissue in a line of an arabesque, a line of expression, a gesture of longing, of openness. There is a demand to be present, which is an excitement in itself. To be steady, to be secure with balance, to know that the steadiness comes from accumulated hours and days of going to classes and seeing them through, of staying with an exercise when the interest fails or attention wanders, this is a victory, a very personal success that goads one to reach for more.

I am grieving. I am confused. I am disorganized. But I stand up with a clear regard for myself. It's not so bad.

I'm letting the debris pile up in the house again. Last night I saw clearly how this messiness keeps me attached to Anatole. The quality of stuckness and inertia and spending days not accomplishing anything keeps me close and still in the empty, sad, terrifying place of husband, lover, friend gone. What do I fear if I move away from that? Losing my connection to Anatole? No, that's not it. Am I afraid of my future? Not exactly. It simply may be that I am choosing to cling to this ledge of sadness with its feeling of being lost. The clinging is who I am right now.

I'm angry and frustrated and worried. When I feel like this, I've always picked up the phone and called a friend, but I can't keep doing that. This is what widowhood is about. There comes a point where you are truly alone with your difficulties. If Anatole were alive, he would say, "Oh, it's not so important. Relax. We can decide tomorrow."

Tonight I sit here and know that the bottom line is that there is no one I can talk to, no one I can turn to when I get an abusive message from a car salesman on my answering machine. There is no one who can tell me, yes, buy a new car that you can't afford, or for economy's sake you will just have to drive your car as it is and learn to put up with its breaking down. The aloneness of all these decisions is difficult to live with. I want to be independent, but the responsibility is daunting.

Twenty-nine years of marriage and then death—it's not like a divorce. It wasn't a decision that my life would be better without Anatole. On the contrary, he and I finally were going to have the time to do things together. Travel, be with friends, get to all the movies we want to see. Not only is there the adjustment of living alone, but it's also the quiet emptiness of his not being here, razor-edged with memories of his suffering. I hate it. I hate what he went through, what he experienced, what I saw and heard. I hate the pain, the physical pain, the terror of it. I hate what the illness did to his body. How in six weeks he could go from dancing to losing the use of his legs. I loved the way Anatole walked. I loved his strut, the way his weight moved through his body. I loved his posture and the vanity of his movement, the timing and agility of his every shift.

I want to scream until my lungs burst. I want my insides to come up through my throat and out of my mouth, for that is what his illness and death have done to me. No, all I want is my husband back, his arms around me, his eyes fastened on mine.

We come around a curve in Bobbie's white Acura and in the distance on the other side of the lake is Kripalu Center for Yoga & Health, a low, beige institutional-looking building with a squat middle tower. My heart sinks. I am to be dropped off there by my best friend from high school with whom I've just spent an easy, slack, indulgent day looking at antiques, talking with her friends, eating breakfast and lunch out. I'm suddenly doubtful and scared about my decision to spend a week in a program called "Quest for the Limitless You." No definite or indefinite modifier before the name. Is the word *quest* a noun or a verb?

Today I've been in beautiful houses with elegant furnishings, and now I shiver knowing that I'm to spend the next seven days in a cement-walled building that resembles a minimum-security prison. It comforts me to know that I've brought a patchwork quilt and colorful sheets from home.

Bobbie helps to carry in my luggage and then leaves abruptly, knowing that I'm miserable and that if she lingered, I'd turn on my heels and get back into her car and go skiing tomorrow. The woman at the front desk gives me endless instructions punctuated with beaming smiles. She knows I'm flustered, so she insists on walking me over to the bulletin boards and then escorting me to the elevator, turning me in various directions to show me how to get to my room once I reach the seventh floor.

In the small room, a monk's cell, for Kripalu was built as a monastery, I unpack and make my bed. I have the sheets that were on Todd's bed when he was a little boy, with their border of choo-choo trains, a pieced quilt from my brother's house, and a pillow with a blue-and-white flannel case from my own bed. I ruminate with my associations to each of these things and then remember with a start that, perhaps, this might be the pillow and pillowcase that I'd brought to Dana Farber and, perhaps, this might be the pillow and pillowcase that were beneath my husband's head when he died. I feel myself sinking into that time, that place, that other small room with cinder-block walls over which I hung quilts and paisley shawls, that other small room with its metal furniture where my husband died. Once again I'm in the room where he suffered, where I leaned over him and cried and kissed his brow, where when the telephone rang I took it into the small bathroom, stretching the cord, so I could tell his friends that he was dying. I didn't want him to hear. I couldn't say to him, Anatole, do you know you're dying? Do you know that we're being separated, that your body is betraying you and me, and that neither I, nor you, nor all of these doctors and nurses and technicians can do anything to stop this?

Here I am sitting on a narrow bed in a monk's cell, tears sliding down my cheeks, missing you, knowing that if you were alive I wouldn't be here. I'd be at home fixing dinner, feeding the dogs, bantering with you or perhaps furious at you for being impatient or sharp-tongued with me. I miss you so much and I miss so much what we have been robbed of. Recently I came across a line in a book that suggests that we are affected by the lives we don't live.

Now off to a silent dinner.

The routine is this. Out of bed at 5:15 a.m. A sleepy walk down the hall to the showers. Make your bed. A silent ride down the elevator to the main meeting room, formerly the monks' chapel, which looks like a Gothic chancel reinterpreted by a 1930s futurist architect. Soaring walls. Clerestory windows. Industrial carpet on the floor. No pews or chairs, for this is where the Kripalu supplicants do their meditation and yoga. Every morning begins with meditation from 5:45 to 6:15, followed by an hour of yoga.

My legs are uncomfortable in the yoga postures. I can't really meditate. I keep thinking about the fear during Anatole's illness. How we or I or he couldn't acknowledge or talk about it. What couldn't we talk about? His death, his loss of life, his lost opportunities, his not writing his books, what our loss would be. Those things between us not said, not done, did that make him sad? Did he ever sense my fear of being alone, of supporting myself, of being adrift, my fear of everything, everything changing?

When I try to focus on my breathing I go back to Anatole's final slow breaths and the painful feelings of that last day. On one hand, I was worn out watching his suffering and I wanted his ordeal to be over. On the other, I am such a believer that I wouldn't let go of hope even though I knew that my expectations were growing smaller and smaller. I was at home sleeping through the night as Anatole's life slowly seeped out of him. The nurses kept saying that many patients need to die alone. Earlier there had been so many people visiting that it was almost a party on those weekends before the seizure. Were there words unsaid? But that thought is stupid because of course there are always words unsaid.

A tinkling bell sounds faintly, signaling the end of meditation. Eyes slowly open, bodies unfold, some stand, some lie on their backs, some move around silently in the ten-minute pause before yoga.

My friend Rosemary, who has attended many workshops here, had told me about Tripti, a massage therapist, who can knead and talk you through hidden layers of psychic pain. She worked on me today, but there were no tears, no release of emotional tension. Rosemary had said that she had cried as memories surfaced. When Tripti pressed certain points and said, "It's rising to meet me. I can feel it," I asked what was rising. She said, weeping to herself, "That's a good question," and then didn't answer it. Was something there? Am I just too defended or obstinate? If the deep probing of the masseuse's thumb connected with internal pain and injuries, I didn't sense it.

This morning in a Quest exercise I had the experience of standing alone on top of a mountain. There was only room for one foot to stand. My back leg was quivering. I was told to stay with the quiver. I was afraid I'd fall. I was told that the fear and the quiver were energy. When I made adjustments, stretching and straightening my arms, putting weight on my back leg and taking a wider stance, I gained more stability.

When you're grateful you're graceful. States of grace always lead to new demands. Become receptive to the gift through giving. Search for new challenges. If you get what you want, it's not right. What you demand is always what you perceive as your deficiency. Achieving what you want doesn't make you who you are. Consider the state of receiving versus the state of achieving. Being grateful leads to relaxation, which opens up a life of celebration. This is New Age philosophy à la Kripalu. The words pull me in, but I don't really know what they mean.

Something's here that I don't like. Shades of Kool-Aid and cults and mindless happiness. In the front hall there is a table with propped-up photographs of Gurudev, Kripalu's CEO, bracketed by candles. Nearby a lounge has rows of Naugahyde chairs, half of them occupied, facing a TV monitor that runs nonstop tapes of Gurudev preaching his wisdom and philosophy. There is a lack of texture, no toughness or hardness, with all these needy people who crave acceptance, self-esteem, love, care. There's no edge, little style, and minimal aesthetics. Would I feel different in a Catholic monastery? Probably, yes. I may need more traditional aspirations for transformation. There needs to be more of a struggle. These are serious matters—one's spirit, right living, the path. Kripalu feels like a panacea. I do not want what they have.

More New Age philosophy. When you are hurt, painful feelings remain inside your body and it's your job to sense and integrate these feelings. We store all over our body. Limitless—means full, experiencing the moment, the truth. If one can stay with the feeling that's feared, then that feeling changes. The energy changes as we enter it. When an upsetting event happens it produces a lot of energy in our body. There is a maximum peak of intensity and then it levels off and calms down.

Breathe. Relax. Feel. Soften the body. Witness. The payoff at the top of the crest is the lesson . . . the "aha" . . . then realization, insight, knowledge. Ride the wave.

All these exercises, switching back and forth from thoughts to feelings to sensations in the body, are a kind of spinning, a disorientation. Everyone is so desperate for solace, including me, that I can't decide if this work is fracturing or healing.

Today there was a presentation of Phoenix Rising Yoga Therapy, which is bodywork that combines yoga postures with emotional exploration.

The body is not as slippery as the mind. Use the body as a vehicle for discovery. What sorts of stories are we carrying around? The body can be a vehicle for change. We're here in life to do it better. Life is a schoolroom. Fear is contraction, and love is expansion. As we move, the pelvis tilts like a bowl. Do we let energy spill out or do we tighten and hold back? Density is energy drawn to the center as in a stomach gripped with fear. With awareness there's a potential for change. Left and right represent the two sides of us, same with back and front. What parts want to go forward and what back? Twisting postures mix the energies. Note a difference, exaggerate it, and then invert it. One can set up a dialogue between the two parts. Find new ways of being, new postures to stretch into. We resist change because the new way is dangerous while our old ways are known and safe.

The last morning is scheduled for rebirthing. By following a sequence of breathing patterns, we are told, one can get to a place of primal associations and feelings. The purpose is to release stress and trauma. The group is split into pairs. Eddy, a psychologist from Pennslyvania, is my partner. We are instructed in the technique of circular breathing. As you lie on your back, deep continuous breaths and exhalations are the means of transport back to or down to early somatic memories. I don't go back to my birth, instead I sense ugliness and contortion around my mouth and constriction on the left side of my body. Isolated itches become torture. I resist scratching. Thoughts of *The Shakers,* a Doris Humphrey dance based on Shaker ritual that I had reconstructed years ago from dance notation, come to mind. In that dance it was the shaking movement of hands that exorcised sin. Then a wave and I'm breathing, gasping, because I'm under a blanket and pillow. It's Anatole's death . . . tears and heaving. I'm covering my face . . . wanting Anatole back and to be held . . . grief that Todd and Bliss can't be held by Anatole anymore. I realize that Eddy is holding and rocking me as I'm sobbing.

Jonathan, a young writer from New York, says at the end of the morning: I'll just sit in gratitude and terror simultaneously.

After a week of yoga, meditation, raw emotions, many tears, I drive back to Cambridge from the Berkshires, wondering if my horizons have changed. I had signed up for this week of trying to find the "limitless me," because of a new friend from Utah, Barbara Jensen, who is doing intensive healing work to combat a recent diagnosis of lymphoma. We shared a room there. Barbara, a rodeo barrel racer from Salt Lake City, went whole-hog with the program. She's headed back West to the vast landscapes of desert and mountain. I'm driving east into the glare of the morning sun, squinting against the brightness, narrowing my eyes, straining to see what's really there.

I need the title to the gray Dodge Caravan so I can pick up the new car. Another salesman at another dealership convinced me I could afford a new car. This is the day after Kripalu. I have a bad cold, with a runny nose and a fever. I'm achy and sad about leaving the gray van, all its history, memories. We got it after the yellow Jeep burned and melted. Some years ago back in Connecticut, when Bliss was in high school, she was driving a group of friends around one afternoon. Smoke began to spew out from under the dash. Wisely someone said, "Hey stop. Let's get out," just before the car became engulfed in flames. The cause was an electrical fire. The insurance adjuster in Hartford was a fan of Anatole's writing. We received twice the worth of the car. We were able to buy a new car, the somber gray van that transported our life in two moves.

I can't find the title. I begin to look in the attic through boxes where there are reminders of nonstop pressures. Old rental agreements for the Vineyard house, school bills, medical bills, miscellaneous receipts, letters never answered, boxes to be sorted, memories to be faced, but not today. The low-grade fever makes my body a misery to me. I think of how Anatole's body shot up to 103 and 104 and I want to know what he felt, what he experienced. The thought of his body heating up and hurting pierces deep, deep inside me.

On the news there is a story about an eighty-three-year-old woman, Jean Yawkey, the Red Sox owner, fighting for her life after a stroke. What does that mean, fighting for her life? I remember how the nurses and doctors would work to stabilize Anatole and then tuck him in and leave. There was a certain diurnal timing in his hospital care. We do this and this and this, and then when the pulse is normal or blood pressure is normal or temp down, we clean up, tuck in, and leave you alone, supposedly to rest, to fight for your life, but there was a sense of abandonment, a turning away, a withdrawal of interest once all the doing was over. It's not the way with doctors today to just be there and attend, to sit and wait and observe, to have a passive interest or curiosity the way psychoanalysts have.

In Western medicine the patient is not totally present for the caregiver. As treatment is administered, the patient is seen as just so much protoplasm whose task and only ability is to respond to the medical interventions.

There must be a better way to help or cure or at least improve a condition. One where the whole range of human aliveness and human response is considered. If there were fuller engagement on both sides, the treatment might be more effective.

Kripalu, for all its faults, reaches for the whole person. The physical, the metaphysical, the spiritual and emotional aspects of one's experience are acknowledged. In class, Marcus once talked about how he wanted a doctor to appreciate his soft tissue. I don't know what soft tissue is anatomically, but I imagine it to be the in-between, not so important, rather shy aspects of our physical self, something that on its own doesn't have a specific responsibility but rather just sustains and cushions and eases all that we demand of ourselves. I imagine that this soft tissue has grown out of quiet times, reading a book, taking a walk alone, being cradled to sleep, making moss gardens in the woods. I imagine that this soft tissue is at work when we rest and when we sleep.

This past year the children moved back home, Todd to save money as he starts a new business and Bliss so she could have her own place. She took over the basement apartment after my first tenant moved out. It's good that we are together again. We need the comfort and contact and rubbing of shoulders, the sprawling on the floor with the dogs. We need the security and knowledge, trust and cooperation of one another. We need to know and experience that we are a family that still has soft tissue.

This from a *Boston Globe* review of *Children of Paradise* about the end of the movie. "The pain on his face as his body strains toward the ever-elusive Garance stands for the suspension in which the film itself is steeped—frozen, eternally poised between consummation and flight, like all timeless romances. Garance's frank stare into the camera reminds us that happy endings are banal, that unfinished business is what keeps love alive."

A few days before Anatole died, the doctor and nurse from radiology, who had treated the skeletal pain from the cancer, came up to the twelfth floor at Dana Farber for a visit. Anatole was not able to talk but could sense visitors. They saw him briefly, after which I walked them back down the hall to the elevators, saying I was most saddened by the realization that Anatole hadn't had the time to finish the books he had planned. Both the nurse and doctor said, But that is the best way to end a life, to be in the middle of unfinished work. For then you are truly alive.

Last night in dreams I was aware of the betrayal of one's body and how that feels when an illness like cancer occurs. I am so invested in my body, I so desperately need it to fully function, that I don't know if I have the capacity to accept the wear and tear and accidents of time. I don't care about the surface. It's the inner workings that are important to me. And I know Anatole also had this body narcissism and so again I awaken to the sense of his profound tragedy—the tragedy of his body virtually imploding on him.

In class today Marcus told someone, "Don't keep your energy locked in your heart." In class the work is to repattern the effort.

Nurse Log

When I leave New England Memorial Hospital on Fridays in the dim winter twilight I often see pairs of Canada geese on the grass near the parking lot. A large reservoir on the other side of a busy road draws them to this suburban area. Today there are three couples. One of the females is eating grass, and her mate is a few feet away keeping a vigil, on the lookout for any danger. I watch their interaction. It is minimal in its movements but intense in its awareness, one of the other. When one makes an adjustment the other notices and immediately makes a compensatory shift. To an insensitive eye these changes in direction of the body, of the head, might seem random, but I know differently for this is a couple mated for life, and I had mated for life and had known and experienced, as one does when one knows that the marriage is for life, that the shifts and gestures need only be small. The intimacy of the relationship becomes this fine essence, a distillation of the earlier passion, but just as powerful. In the marriage that endures there is no need for grandiosity. There is a privacy in the barely noticeable word or shoulder shift. It's almost mind reading. I miss the finesse of all that.

From a long history of coupleness I am adjusting to the oneness. This is a maneuver from the mutuality of the duet to being solo, a single person, only intimate with myself, tuning in on my own small shifts and tolerating my larger tumult.

I realize that now I'm not talking to others about this aloneness. The deadness, the desolation is too strong to be verbalized. I would have to yell, use profanity, tear the clothes off myself to give a sense of what this is, this loss of a husband, of a brother, of security, feeling naked and alone in the world, wanting to stay naked and alone in the world, having lost the fear of homelessness because that is meaningless next to the memory of my husband's slow death and the sense of my brother's body suddenly turning cold and gray on a summer afternoon. If my words are melodramatic it's only that they are necessary for myself, to see on paper what rumbles in my heart.

Today, almost eighteen months later, I don't believe he's gone, that he could have died so quickly. Anatole was ripped out of my life, ripped out of his life. I don't want to pat and make smooth this open wound. I am reminded of the upended trees we saw in Dorset two years ago, roots torn from the earth, great gashes in the earth, crater-like depressions, deep holes, dead bark, rotting branches. In the forest the fallen tree becomes a nurse log and gives birth to new life. The fracturing, the raw hurt of loss in itself may be the way of healing, of continuing to live. This writing could be a part of the way. I could write myself into a new life or at least a new place past where I am now, except I don't want to leave this loss, my husband's death. It is my strongest sensation of him now.

I examine my face in the mirror. I see how gravity pulls my skin down, separating it from inner flesh, turning it gray, causing it to drape into wrinkles. I notice this downward pull with its somber demeanor and am amused that I don't find it upsetting.

There were times that Anatole was alone when he was in the hospital. Before Dana Farber he was at the Brigham sharing a room with a man who couldn't talk because of a wired jaw. Anatole passed the time reading *The Transit of Venus*, so entranced that he was able to see his illness as a multihued fan, delicate and quivering like the spreading of a peacock's tail, instead of just fear and pain. That is what he wrote in the flyleaf of the book. Multihued feathers and fallen trees, images from nature that are consoling, that get one through.

The nurse log, I do this well, the staying still and prone, heavy with my own weight and debris. Today the pain of losing my husband and brother feels like a gagging void that I want to retch up and out. I want to vomit my emptiness and smear it all over the floor, the walls, windows, over anyone who is within reach. I want to make the void, the aloneness, visible, tangible, to be touched, smelled. I want people to recoil from it, to know its stench, its putridness, the way it eats away and corrodes what is nice and comfortable. It frightens me to be alone with the mess of my life, the losses of my life. I sit here and hold on to my two dogs and my cat. I don't know if I'm holding on to myself. Must grief be silent? I know that my grief is mostly private.

I was invited to dinner tonight at the Hulsizers' with Sherif and Mary Nada. Throughout the evening I noticed the affection in their marriages, solid and loving marriages. Bob Hulsizer talked about the possibility of cruising in the Caribbean. Did we want to go? Don't know if the invitation extended to me. I'm not sure if I could or would want to go along as a single woman. This makes me wonder about when and where I am to be excluded, and if it will be I or others who will keep me apart.

Sunday. Stayed in the house all day, remembering Sundays when Anatole and I were at home. He would become restless.

He would need to get out, take a walk, do something, and we would, and it would be a relief not to be stuck with one's own dead ends, musty and stale.

I've known this feeling for most of my life. I can remember, as a child of eight or ten, going downstairs to an empty kitchen in the afternoon in a silent house. I would open a cream-painted cabinet door and peer inside, not knowing what I wanted to find. Sometimes I would start baking.

Without Anatole this house is overly quiet in all its corners. Sunday continues to have an uneasiness to it. My restless qualms are a kind of allegiance to Anatole, to feel what he might have felt today, this second day of spring with its gray cold loyalty to winter. I could take a walk, but the dogs nested in their dog beds near the radiators seem disinclined, or that is how my leaden mind sees them, a misperception surely for they have no Sunday neurosis and always bound up for a walk.

Today I told my friend Jessica, who suffers from a painful childhood, "Don't expect to get over it." It will always be there, and if you think that it will go away you'll be disappointed. So learn to live with it—the loss, the hurt, the memories, the anguish. Become familiar with the roar in your head. Know that from time to time you will be pushed off balance, but keep agile and then you won't be hurt in the falls. If you do hurt yourself, get some first aid and go on. Know that there's a possibility of being reasonably happy even though the shadows and darkness stay. They will never disappear, nor would I have it that way. Like an alcoholic in recovery I must remember to touch, taste, feel my anguish every day to keep myself alive. If I stop doing this, some part of me will have died and the deadness will spread like my husband's cancer and catch me unawares, and then I might break apart or go mad. The way of my life now is not to put Anatole's and Brook's deaths behind me but to stay with them, carry their deaths with me. Put their ashes in my pocket, rub their grit between my fingers. Use their remains as my touchstone, my rabbit's foot, my guide.

Writing helps. My thoughts are so much more precious to me than my actions or activity. Writing is cozy, it's private. In losing Anatole I've lost the cozy and private part of my life and oddly enough I rediscover it with pencil and paper. I don't feel alone when I write. I am with myself.

I wonder. What are my prospects? How will I survive?

Breathe. See it through.

At the urging of a friend I attend a Feldenkrais workshop given by Josef Della Grotte. We spend the day applying the principles of the Feldenkrais technique to some basic yoga postures. Instead of moving any which way into the yoga positions, the instructor shows us how to consciously shift into the postures using our weight and sensing bones and joints.

Joseph has been teaching Feldenkrais for many years. His personality is like his favorite dance, the tarantella, and words tumble out of his mouth with the same spirited joy as the dance.

Fitness is not health.

You can accomplish stuff and ruin yourself.

Explore and learn with awareness.

If the body is tense then the mind will jump around.

Goal is for equanimity first and then transformation.

Peace first and then God.

Less entropy and more organization leads to less aging.

Goal is to improve functioning.

Earlier in the week I had landed the wrong way in dance class and had bruised my heel and was noticeably limping. I ask Joseph about this. He has me walk across the room while his hands are on my lower back making a slight adjustment in the tilt of my hips. By the end of the day the pain is gone. Finding an easier way to move, a way that is without strain and without discomfort, may be possible.

. . .

As I drive through Falmouth and then around the series of downhill curves that lead to Woods Hole, I sense behind my back and on the edge of my peripheral vision all the trips that we as a family have made over this road before. Exhausted from packing up our Connecticut house, which was rented each summer, we would be relieved that we were making the boat on time, and expectant, knowing what lay in front of us—a summer of beach, friends, dancing, tennis, reclaiming our bodies and ourselves. It's not as if we didn't appreciate those years. We did. We knew they were good years even as we complained and worried and hassled ourselves and others. We knew we'd made good choices in one another, in places to live.

I don't cry anymore driving to Woods Hole. I just feel sad. The tears have sunk to just beneath the surface. There are no drops sliding down my cheeks, but just underneath my skin like a hair shirt that's been inserted between the epidermis and fascia layers of my body there is a raw sensation of aloneness that keeps reminding me and repeating to me, I am bereft, I am bereft. With the slowest of slowed-down motion, grief is moving from the surface to my center, like a stone sinking slowly to the bottom of the ocean floor. Last summer there were tears, and the permissible private wail. Now it is this sensation that stays with me all the time, an internal sadness that sets me apart, makes me inaccessible in certain ways for others. It will become different as it moves toward my center.

In public I often find myself responding to shopkeepers, cashiers, ticket takers with a vivacity that is not me. It's as if I'm frantically practicing for the time when I'm old and unsavory but realize that people will still respond to me if I have an upbeat tone. This chirpy voice is not me. Am I that scared?

Tonight I wrote to a friend saying that out of crisis and upheaval strengths develop, a social work dictum. I told her this because I don't want her to be concerned about me, but I don't really believe that. I don't know what skills I've gained other than an unpleasant ability to see through some bullshit and an awareness that platitudes are just that, platitudes. Does being crippled, ill, or poor have its rewards? No. The same with death and losses and grief. They are in the minus column of life. They do not lead to enlightenment, only sadness. Life is unequal in its distribution of wealth and of tragedy.

Right now it seems to me that I've been left on the dock, so to speak, as others sail off—like the time when I was ten years old in Gothenburg, Sweden. My grandmother, mother, and older sister and I were sailing home on the SS *Gripsholm* after spending two months in Europe. In the confusion of customs and boarding the ship I became separated from my family. The boat was sounding its departure with long sequential blasts from its horns and I was walking wildly around on the dock approaching strangers, none of whom spoke English, trying to find a way to board the boat. The gangplank had been taken away. I became hysterical, and an English-speaking officer was found. Politeness and composure had not worked. I did get on board, and when I found my mother and sister, they did not seem to see or recognize how panicked I had been. Perhaps I didn't tell them. Earlier on that same trip I had become separated from them on the top of the Jungfrau in Switzerland.

Near the crest of the mountain there was a large tourist complex with a restaurant and gift shops. Carved out under the surface of a glacier were ice rooms and a skating rink. After lunch the same thing had happened. I couldn't find my family. For two hours I searched for them, pacing between the main lobby and the empty frozen ice rooms, one with a carved ice table and low backless ice chairs around it. Everyone had disappeared. As it turned out, there had been two tours on two different cable cars that took sightseers farther up the mountain. My mother and grandmother had gone on one while my sister was on the other, each assuming that I was with the other. When these tours returned and I found my mother, grandmother, and sister, they didn't understand how lost and frightened I had been. To them it was a silly misunderstanding. This time, also, I hadn't told them. I didn't have the words or the emotional repertoire to let them know what it had been like for me, a child, to have wandered in and out of empty frozen rooms for those two endless hours.

I used to think that if I'd ever been psychoanalyzed these two events would have provided critical material, but now I see them as harbingers of what was to follow in my life. Separation and panic. The difference now is that finally I have found the words to tell of the experience.

Bliss was looking at the linen jackets in the Tweeds catalogue at the kitchen table today. Two years ago in Paris Anatole and I picked out a navy blue linen jacket for her at Kenzo. She was home taking care of the dogs. I remember Anatole, sicker than I knew, needing to take naps. I couldn't sit in the hotel room quietly and read while he rested. I had to get out. Walking down rue Grenelle I realized that I was practicing walking alone, testing it out, glancing sideways at shop windows to notice my reflection, alone, as a single woman, knowing that our time as a couple was limited. Standing on a corner, waiting for traffic, for the light to change, I choked back tears, for there was no arm or hand at my side to pull me back if I were to impulsively start across without looking, which would often happen when I was with Anatole.

I'd always known that we were a striking couple, but now, alone, I was invisible, a nonentity. I suddenly felt old. I wanted to turn back, but where could I go? Not back to the hotel room. If I returned I would have to wake Anatole and reassure myself of his aliveness, but I didn't want to disturb him. He needed his rest. I walked on, forcing my steps, concentrating on keeping my back straight, wiping away the few tears that slid down past my clenched jaw. Even though I continued to hope at this point that Anatole was going to live for quite a while, some part of me, an ugly remorseless part, knew he wouldn't, and that part was forcing me forward to new and strange streets.

Nurse Log

I have always been independent and have done lots of things alone and am content with my own company, but to be alone when you know that somewhere there is another heart, another being who is a familiar part of your life, is very comfortable. Then it's a choice or a plan to be alone. Perhaps something needs doing that's better done alone, a chore, a project. But to be alone because there is no one else in another room, another town, another place who occasionally thinks of you is to be alone in a random unconnected way. To be alone like this means a life or a day with no edges. If I get home late or I don't get home at all, who will notice?

I heard an anecdote on NPR. Sometime in February the frozen body of an elderly woman was discovered on a chair in a recessed alcove on a balcony high in an apartment building in Stockholm. She was bundled in warm clothes. Evidently she had a heart attack on New Year's Eve while watching the fireworks.

As I walked down those Parisian streets, perhaps there were ice crystals forming on the inner side of my spine.

There are memories and then there are dreams. Most have been long and meandering. Wandering, being lost in familiar places. Collages of what is known and what is foreign. Dissolves, as in films from my childhood home, my parents there, to people and places I know now. I have awoken from them with sadness. In recent weeks my dreams have become more difficult. In one my Cambridge house was being remodeled. Standing on the sidewalk with my friend Gwindale, I realized that all the walls, everything had been torn down. There was nothing left.

Last night's dreaming was gut-wrenching. Earlier in the evening I had gone to a dinner at the Millers' with Isidor and Hunt and the Polsters. Two years ago in early April there had been an identical evening with the same people, except now Anatole wasn't there. That's all I was aware of the whole evening, the face that was not there, the anecdotes that weren't told.

In the dream Anatole's body had been cut into pieces. He had been sawed across the chest at the sternum. I don't know how or why but his head and chest were placed in a cupboard, like our old jelly cupboard, on a shelf on the left side at a height of four feet, and we were waiting for him, for Anatole, to die so we would close the door and go away, but then we would come back and find that he was still alive. At one point I was alone opening the cupboard doors. The head had begun to be puffed and distorted and changed in a terrible way as in a horror movie, and Anatole's hands, which hadn't been there before, were placed on either side of his forehead. I was horrified by what he had to endure. When we checked again, Anatole, his head and neck and only the barest part of his upper chest, had moved and were on a lower shelf on the right side, the other side, of the cupboard. There were some other people around. I don't know who they were. Had they moved Anatole's head there? Well, the head now looked more normal, more like Anatole. I bent over his head with mine, as I had done with my father when he was dying, to say how much I loved him. He looked at me, perhaps his eyes weren't open, but I know he sensed me and said something or reassured me in some way. I remember him talking; it's just that I didn't hear the words. Then the phone rang. I woke up.

I've been haunted all day. This is the first time in a dream that Anatole and I have had contact. He has been present in other dreams but only as a background figure.

The ghoulish face must be a visual image of my grief, together with the visceral missing of Anatole that I carry inside. I wonder if I had died how would he feel. Would he have found someone else right away? Would he have remembered me? Did he know how important he was to me? I have this sense that I know more about how much I meant to him, how much I provided for him, a home, a family, a life, domesticity, than he knew himself. And I don't mind that he didn't know.

. . .

Anatole's book has arrived. *Intoxicated by My Illness.* The solidity and heft of the package, the weight and shape of the book in my hand, were like another shipment of ashes. My husband's remains, neatly labeled, identified, tied up, squared off, contained, a neat product is all that is left. For days now the book rests on the dining room table. I am dragging myself around. I have the image of being alone on a gray, leaden sea. Anatole has fallen overboard. He has drowned. His body, his familiar face sink slowly to the floor of the ocean. I have dropped the lines and the tiller. I sit in the boat occasionally making an empty gesture. The sails luff, the hull bobs. We, the boat and I, have no way. If I held on to the sails and the rudder, I would begin to sail away, but I don't do that. I stay here like a dog who is faithful and has lost his master and waits for years at the spot where he last saw the person he loved.

Last weekend on the Vineyard, I had the earthquake dream. I fell into a fissure of a quake. Quicksand, like slime, closed over me. I sank down. I was about to die and then I was up on a cracked bit of firm ground. That's the sequence. Death, oblivion, and then the earth, support once more—like the Graham fall, where you collapse in a spiral path to the floor then release back, sinking into the ground only to arch your back to the point where you are forced to do a whiplike contraction that brings you up to your feet, standing in an open lunge with head and chest straining for the sky.

The next day in class Marcus told me that I can relax more when I'm going at a fast tempo, that I don't need the extra tension and energy. He went on about relying on the short hairs of the middle ear for maintaining the speed. For the first time in a long time I stayed to the end of the class. In *Women Who Run with the Wolves,* Clarissa Pinkola Estés says don't wait to do something for the time when you will be less afraid, because the fear will always be there. So I stayed and we did a wonderful, awkward, Duncanesque dying phrase with a drunken fall and angry tosses. Marcus said it's crucial to know what to release, what not to hold on to in order to move, what to let go of, what to get rid of. I want to dance. I want to sing, and to do this I've got to clear out my life, so why do I hold on to the chaos, the mess, the debris? I must want both, the moving and the rubble. On Monday Bill Costanza, my dance teacher on the Vineyard, said I should still be performing. Why should I want to do that at my age? But I do. I want to fly, be expressive, fling myself against the horizon.

The Second Cancer

The second summer without Anatole begins. Each week I leave Cambridge on Friday for the Vineyard and return on Monday. Today, I arrive at Woods Hole at 3:05 and get right on the *Nantucket,* the boat with the three-place sofa-like passenger seats that have no interrupting arm-rests. Anatole would find an empty one near a bathroom and lie down, close his eyes, and have a private struggle with the nausea. These thoughts are less painful now than when remembered last summer.

A sense of sadness comes and goes these days. When I'm working in the Vineyard garden I sense it, the aloneness, with its clammy, musty feel just on the edge of tears. I go on with whatever I'm doing when I have this feeling.

This morning in dance class Marcus said I was getting up on my legs. That's good. These stronger muscles I'm developing keep me vertical, keep me walking.

Yesterday Bliss had a hard day. There was a mistake in the month-end statements for which she was responsible. She cried at the office and continued to cry at home. She feels overwhelmed by her job and fears the stress will get worse. Later at night she was in bed sobbing. She's afraid she's falling apart. I lay down next to her and held her and stroked the long muscles of her back and legs. I told her I loved her. She fears that I could die too. When she gets overwhelmed, she misses her father terribly. So do I.

Barbara, my friend from Utah, has arrived. We will be joined by her shaman, River, for a long weekend on the Vineyard. I met Barbara last September at the Wellness Week in Utah. Several people from that program, including Barbara, had had sessions with River, a massage therapist who works with your psyche as she kneads your muscles. Barbara, who lives in Salt Lake City, continued to see River and tells amazing stories about her shamanic talents and the "inner vision quests" that she does with her clients.

We pick up River at South Station. Her tanned face is framed in the rearview mirror. Flashes of green eyeliner behind dark-blue sunglasses. Long unmatched earrings. She makes sudden strong gestures in the car, pointing to birds, trees, her eyes all-seeing.

She tells the story of a man who couldn't smell, a thirty-something, fast-track New Yorker who came to her after a day of nonstop downhill skiing at Snowbird. River begins her vision quest by consulting Sirius, a spirit who sees the client through River. Sirius tells the story of an Indian tribe and how they hunted. The women went out first and negotiated with the animals for their needs. Then the animals would present gifts to be given to the tribe. The hunters would appear. The rule was to always kill the second animal seen, because the first might be the last. When the white man came, the Indian culture fell apart. A young man who'd been a wolf hunter was used as a tracker by the white men. The ways of hunting had changed and negotiations no longer were held. Wolves were killed randomly with no plan. Hides were taken. The rest of the animal was left to rot. The young hunter whose job it was to track by smelling the paths of the wolves began to drink. One day in a drunken brawl the bridge of his nose where the olfactory nerves are was smashed and he died. He had never grieved the loss of his community and its ways. Instead he drank.

At each point in the story River kept asking the driven New Yorker, "Does this seem true to you? Do you want to go on?" The implication was that now, perhaps, he could do the grieving about what he had lost in his race for success and retrieve those missing parts of himself. River then had the client lower his head. She finds a point of entrance and blows the fragmented piece of soul back into him.

As she tells the story of the young man who can't smell I wonder what questions I would ask of her. I'm always misplacing things. Does this include bits of myself? Have I lost parts of myself and don't know it?

On the ride down to Woods Hole, River and I talk about our professions and their differences. We talk of how we work. I tell her about one of my patients, an elderly woman, Vivian, who speaks only of sadness, anger, and being misunderstood. Yet there is a fabric and grace to her life as she tells of her garden, as she acknowledges the caring in the brusque manner of her husband of forty-eight years. River says her work is 50,000 years old. Can we trust each other? I tell her I would like to write an article about her, and I see a question in her eyes. Am I the person to write about her? She suggests a magazine, *Women with Power.* I resist. I tell her I'm not on that wavelength. I'm not angry. River tells me I come from a place of privilege. I disagree. We spar. She apologizes. I say it's okay. Perhaps I am angry.

I ask her how she became a shaman. It began with an eight-year vision-quest experience in her late teens and twenties. River, née Leslie Sterling, said she knew she wanted to work with souls.

The first morning on the Vineyard is clear and cool. The

sun's warmth is tempered by brisk wind. I check my answering machine in Cambridge. There is a message to call the doctor who ten days ago had done a cone biopsy. The Pap test last October was clean, but my doctor felt that it was wise to recheck this spring, because in the past three years I had had two slightly irregular Pap results.

I return the doctor's call. She wants to schedule me for a hysterectomy. The result of the cone biopsy, which is the removal of a small wedge-shaped piece of tissue from the cervix, was that I have squamous-type cancer cells. This category of cancer cells means that the disease has not burrowed deep into surrounding tissue. The treatment is to remove the cervix and the uterus. Follow-up chemotherapy will probably not be necessary.

I sit on the tall wooden kitchen stool, elbows on the counter, head down, trying to hear every syllable, every nuance, every shading of the doctor's voice. I can tell that she is uncomfortable giving me this information over the phone, but since I am going to be away for a few days, she doesn't want to wait to schedule the operation. I ask and ask again the same questions, writing down the words I hear, asking how to spell them. My mind, my brain sputters, like a car running out of gas. An involuntary shivering begins in my head, my chest, my arms. River and Barbara are ten feet away sitting in chairs on either side of the woodstove, their heads bowed over books. Ten months earlier, when I had met Barbara in Utah, she had just been diagnosed with lymphoma and had decided to pursue alternative treatment after I had told her about Dr. Gonzalez in New York.

When I hang up the phone River and Barbara steady me by asking rational, factual questions so we can sort out the information I have received. They suggest a walk on the beach. South Beach here in Chilmark is remarkably beautiful and has a range of moods and tides. It is wide and expansive, with sandy dunes and long horizons, as well as sculptural, with large boulders in the water and on the beach. Along one stretch there are multicolored clay cliffs. It is a landscape that always fills me with peace and pleasure. Walking quiets my shivering. River offers to do a soul retrieval and an alternative diagnosis according to Chinese medicine. Any alternative is appealing.

Todd and Bliss join us on Friday night. They bond with River. Bliss borrows one of River's elaborate beaded earrings to wear as we leave for the Aquinnah Shop for breakfast on the Gay Head cliffs on Saturday morning. I tell my children about the cancer, and in the same sentence I say that it is nothing to be concerned about. A simple hysterectomy will get rid of it.

I am very calm. I don't want them to see my fear. They need to believe that I am all right, that I won't die on them. None of us wants to look at that possibility. It is too close to their father's death. We are still shaky. Any strong emotion could unbalance us, so we agree to change the subject and instead figure out what to do for the day. Sunday afternoon I put them on the boat back to the mainland. When I return to Abel's Hill, River begins the soul retrieval.

The weather is still cool so we add wood to the stove in the downstairs room, the kitchen at one end, a trestle table at the other, and in between a couch, chairs, and the woodstove. Cushions and a feather bed are placed close to the warmth of the fire, and River gives me a massage. Then she takes pulses at various points of my body, the liver pulse, the kidney and heart pulses. Some of these are weak. To strengthen these organs, River does acupuncture.

The immersion in another person's focus is deeply consoling. My whole being is supported and floating on River's consciousness, her hands, her voice, her being. River sits quietly by my side and closes her eyes and asks my permission to do a soul retrieval. I say yes. She is very still for a few minutes and then begins to tell me about the pieces of my fragmented soul that she has found.

There is a piece from the early years of our marriage that was hurt and alone. Am I ready to take that sad and worried part of me back and take care of it? River has a vision of Bliss, who says that she is willing to return the part of me that she holds. I also am holding on to part of her. Am I ready to exchange these pieces of each other that we, mother and daughter, cling to? River also sees three clients who are demanding and take parts of me. She suggests I build a shield or blue cocoon before each day of work. River tells me to move on in my life. I have a future and so does Anatole. I'm getting paler and thinner. Nothing is coming into my life. It is time to end the vigil.

River lights a smudge stick, sage wrapped with twine, and fragrant smoke snakes around my head and body. Then she places her mouth on the top of my head and blows back the errant pieces that she has found, blows them back into my soul.

This all makes so much more sense to me than the word *cancer,* the illness cancer. Knowing that I am out of balance, that I have been sending too much energy out and not taking in, that it is time to grieve less and live more, that I do not have to cling to my daughter to stay close with her, that it is all right to protect myself from the demands of some clients, knowing, learning all this gives me a map to follow, something concrete to do. I do not have to be passive in the face of the cancer. It is a huge relief.

Getting back to Cambridge, I make the follow-up doctor's appointments. The operation is scheduled for June 23, six weeks away. I continue to see clients in the afternoons and evenings and get to dance classes in the morning. Friends are supportive but I can sense their fear. I tell them and the children that I'll be fine because the cancer was caught so early. I call Dr. Gonzalez in New York and he says, yes, operate, and then he gives me a list of supplements that will help. Outwardly, I'm positive and upbeat but inside there is fear that is becoming amplified because I am alone with this.

It is Tuesday, June 23, seven-thirty in the morning. I'm at the Brigham and Women's Hospital waiting for the operation. There have been many thoughts and fears leading up to this procedure. Going through it alone and yet not alone, I know that I have friends who today are thinking about me. To be back in this hospital where Anatole had surgery is difficult, where we—Todd, Bliss, and I and our friends—spent so many anxious, difficult, frustrating hours.

Three days after the operation Bliss drives me down to the Vineyard. With no stairs to climb it will be easier here to walk the dogs and take care of myself. I can move slowly but am not yet able to drive. Bliss spends an overnight and returns to Boston. Now I'm alone on the Vineyard, staying quiet, being still, beginning to read Proust, wondering how these words were to Anatole as he read them on a ship in the Pacific in 1943 or '44.

Because of this operation my life has stopped. I have stopped. I'm making an effort to stay with the stillness. Thoughts and ideas are beginning to return to me. Most are fleeting and have vanished, for I've not written them down. Perhaps they were thoughts about the operation, about losing a part of myself, or reactions to the fact that Sam, a man I had taken a few walks with, has gotten married.

Do I thirst after a relationship? I don't think so. The thirst is more to stay with myself. To locate my center. To find calmness and order. To create a setting that will help me do my work. I need to learn more about how to live with the sadness.

Before the operation I was filled with fear and apprehension. I hated the loneliness. I drew back into myself, closed my shell, and cried and yearned for Anatole. Now I am snuggling into aloneness, wrapping it about me like a throw, tucking my toes under its edges. I am breathing in, pulling in the world to me and then being still so I can notice what is at my elbow, at my knees, or behind my left shoulder. I want to find out who I am, this fifty-four-year-old woman without a husband, a mother, a father, a brother. To whom and to what am I connected? Do I need to make decisions or changes in my life? How do I go on living in a way that is not simply automatic and assumed? Is there a star to guide me?

To be in this house alone feels right because I am alone. The surroundings fit my reality, and perhaps this is the way to adjust, to find a new shape, a new being that can "go it" alone and not pretend an all-rightness. Perhaps, now, alone, I can discover my own all-rightness. I don't want a salve, a bandage, a label, a stance. I want to change into a new being, have a metamorphosis, shift my structure.

Looking through a box shoved to the side in Bliss's closet I find the sign that she and I came upon in a London flea market while she was in college, spending a semester working and studying there. An oval painted metal sign, never used, with a bird and dune grass underneath the words *Sandy Lodge*. I brought it home and forgot about it. Now, finally, I hang it over the front door.

There was some bleeding after a walk on the beach today. I realize that being alone I can't take chances. If I started hemorrhaging and had to go to the hospital, who would I call?

I'm feeling distant from my friends here. It's summer and they're busy with houseguests and weekend chores.

Am I angry at Suzy for not coming by? Perhaps I am. But too much has gone wrong in my life. My friends have already made too many caretaking visits. What angers me is that no one knows how to help. Come to dinner, they say, four days after the operation. What do they think is going on with me? It's confusing, because I sound and look okay. They have no sense of the cutting and refitting that has gone on inside of me, but perhaps they know that I need to stay still and be sad with my empty pelvis.

My vagina without a uterus is a dead end. Its far edges are sewn together and attached to my abdominal wall. No longer is my vagina an entry to a place beyond. Now it is only a cavity, a burrow. In some cultures despondency is seen as soul loss. Does womb loss bring on melancholia? I will meditate on this emptiness until I find a new definition for this changed part of myself.

I want to change myself along with this change in my body.

My life needs surgery, pruning, a cutting away of useless, potentially cancerous parts. There needs to be more focus, more clarity, less oozing, less randomness.

I was in the bathroom putting on moisturizer. Player was licking my legs, and then George lapped at my ankle too. In her dotage she continues to learn new tricks from Player. I smiled and spoke to her in my silly dog voice and realized that this was a moment of happiness and pleasure. At the same time I sensed that feeling okay was possible. I walked back into our bedroom and was looking in the mirror when the lamp on Anatole's side of the bed, the side I now sleep on, flicked on and off very quickly like a firefly at night. I turned to the lamp and said out loud, "Anatole, you're here. You're with me. You saw what just happened with the dogs. What are you telling me? Is it that you want me to be happy? Is that it? You want me to stop suffering?" And then the light flicked on and off again but this time much more slowly and emphatically, the light being lit for almost a full second. I stood there looking at the light for a few more moments. It was still and dark. I didn't go over to check if it was on or off.

Sitting here in the living room, on the couch, a few moments later, sitting in the place under the broad picture window where Anatole used to read with Jassy lying alongside his thigh, writing these words, I miss him and feel teary, but that passes and I sense a smugness inside of me, knowing that Anatole with his extraordinary spirit and energy is of course with me and watching over me and Todd and Bliss and the pups and even Belle, our other cat. In fact, Jassy is probably right at his side watching too. The tears begin as I see him physically in these rooms once more. I take a deep breath and move back to sensing his spirit, his vitality, his wish for my happiness. A concern for the other's happiness and contentment is an important part of a marriage that survives. To wish the other well. What a simple, civilized, uncomplicated thought. A wish is a message, a communication, a missive that can be sent to another person. Best wishes. Congratulations. These are not empty words. They make a difference, in me, in who I am, in my energy and outlook.

I take a few more deep breaths and notice the sound of the early-morning Vineyard breeze rustling the oak leaves like a musical comb gliding through a green field. I am still and surrounded by Anatole's wish for me. His wish for me to be well. His wish for me to be happy. To continue the contentment and happiness that were the very best part of our marriage. Walking arm in arm through streets in Paris or London or Fairfield or Southport or on South Beach, this was perfect, and that is the legacy of our life together. That remains. And that is Anatole's reminder to me this morning. He reminded me of the strength and goodness of what we knew and of what I can continue to know and have. Happiness and pleasure in existing in this world and noticing and observing the changing panorama of people and landscape.

Dreary cold day. About 60 degrees. Damp, overcast, on the edge of rain. Last night I felt at peace and strong. Today I am sad, depressed, shriveled, deflated, and on the verge of tears like the weather. I'm aware of a clamshell-like response in me. A shutting up and withdrawing from people, annoyed that friends are not calling, not on my doorstep.

Right now I'm angry with Bliss. She arrived with a boyfriend on Thursday night. I picked them up at the ferry, made them dinner and then breakfast the next morning. It's now Saturday morning. Bliss left the garbage out and the dogs tore it apart. I cleaned it up because they were sleeping late. Bliss and her friend have chomped through most of the food in the house. I want to be able to feed her and her friends, but I am worried about money. I want to provide, but the cupboards are bare. It's not only losing Anatole and Brook but I have lost the base of the financial support that I've known most of my life. I sense that my friends don't want to see this. It's too unsettling. They and I collude in seeing all the positive stuff in my life. A bouncy spirit, my many interests, two beautiful children, two houses, a flower garden in bloom. Yes, that's all there, but what is also there, inside, is the pain, the blackness, the quiet, the lack of an intimate relationship, for better or for worse, in my life.

When I am still with this emptiness, there is a piercing feeling of my husband being torn away, leaving raw bleeding flesh with nerve endings that cry out for a new connection. My skin, my flesh yearns for consolation, but there is only stillness and the concreteness of solid objects like chairs, beds, a table, and the daily necessities of eating and sleeping. I rub the arm of the couch where I'm sitting and think back through all the rooms and houses that this couch, acquired twenty-nine years ago, has furnished. All the occasions and ways it was sat upon and used. For dinner parties. Anatole read his books on it. Christmas presents were opened on it. These tangible pieces of a life that was happy remain.

Sunday night, Fourth of July weekend, alone at Sandy Lodge, hearing fireworks off in the distance, reminds me of the years of driving back to Connecticut to return to work on fireworks night, leaving Anatole and the kids on the Vineyard. Like the weekend-commuter husbands of the previous generation, I would make the three-day turnaround trips between work and vacation home.

Driving through Fairhaven, water on the left, I would pull off with other cars and watch alone for five minutes the bursting flowers and umbrellas of light, the soft, slow centrifugal flaring followed by a deep, dull bang. The low boom and the falling cinders, seeing and hearing this from the closed capsule of my air-conditioned car marked the separation from my family. I was fulfilling my responsibilities and obligations by going back to work, but it was a lonely business, that long drive back to Connecticut on a hot summer night.

Tonight, this year, it's cool on the Vineyard, and again I'm alone as I hear the distant thudding of fireworks on the mainland. Earlier this evening I put Bliss and her boyfriend on the six-thirty boat. The distant noise reinforces my aloneness and I'm tempted to call a friend, to get connected, to complain, to listen for empathy, but I don't. I sense that there is something to find in this solitude and quiet. I don't even turn on the radio.

While puttering in the kitchen a thought begins to find a shape like a burst of fireworks in extremely slow motion. The kernel of the detonation that begins ever so slowly is this: Here I am alone in this summerhouse. I don't want any houseguests, and the reason is that to have houseguests without Anatole would be very different. Without Anatole the conversations might be only mediocre. This house that has cradled such ribald and far-flung rhetoric might wither if banality and platitudes seeped in through its shrinking floorboards. Better to stay alone, let the kids have their friends with their youthful energy. I am asking myself to be extraordinary and this is something I can better do alone.

Last summer it was a free-for-all as we buried Anatole's ashes. Suzy and Hugh, Candy and Rick, we all regressed to bathroom and locker talk. But now the burning cinders have fallen, have landed, and are extinguished. The light, the glitter, the life of this house has to find another source.

I have to call the IRS. They've put a lien on my house, probably because I haven't responded to their notices of an overdue tax. All my guilt, queasiness, and uncertainty surface. I'm angry at my stupidity, my procrastination. All this talk, talk, words, words that I do with others and myself. It hobbles me. Better to talk less and just act and get things done, the way Candy does. Go for the immediate solution. Don't think too much. Get it out of the way. Don't listen to the static. Tune it out. Act, don't react. All this worry and mess and disorder is a waste. The stagnation in my life, the inertia, the confusion, the "I can't" stance make me sick.

In pain again. I did too much yesterday. I was really stupid. I brush-cut tall weeds on the hill below the house, pulling and wrestling with the twenty-pound lawn mower that's meant to mow suburban lawns. As my friend Lia says, at the time it seemed like a good idea. Now I hurt inside as if sutures have been ripped and flesh torn apart.

The pain stops me, stills me. I put aside the daily chores. I think about these past two weeks. The solitude, the lack of socializing, being alone with my fears, meditating on the loss of my uterus. I wonder if I have achieved any peace, arrived at any resolution, as in a return or transition to a major key at the end of a piece of music. But to be rigorously honest, I have no new insights, no wisdom, no serenity, only an empty cupboard, and a new sense of bitterness and a few tears. Not the stuff for drama or poetry, the mood is more that of a dirty sink with dishes waiting to be done and a few ants crawling around.

I hope I'll feel better in the morning.

Being alone at home on a Saturday night with two dogs and a cat is my choice, I suppose. The beginning today, I sense for the first time, of being winnowed or widowed out of the couples' world I used to know. At the swap meet, the Shweders and Kreigers, speaking of their evening plans, say over and over again, "Don't come too early, not before eight. Remember. Eight o'clock," while I'm backing away and saying, "Bye, I've got to get going." No one hears or replies.

I am different now. I know it, and others are just beginning to sense it. Stronger, wiser, smarter, I know things they don't. I've seen things they haven't seen. I've persevered. I've endured and they don't quite know who I am. I'm not quite sure myself. I tap a richer vein when I'm alone. I need to explore. The two deaths and now the cancer, these things have changed me. I am more vivacious, and at the same time disturbingly sad and angry—angry that my friends don't see the shifts in me. Instead they label me and others who suffer with clichés and false admiration, with words like courage and strength, and all the while I want to crawl on my hands and knees and howl. I can't be with them easily. They inhabit a world of security and safety that I have left. Theirs is a different language, different assumptions. They would not row backwards to pick up a spider.

On Thursday, leaving *Swallow,* there was a large spider in the dinghy. I tried to put it on *Swallow.* It fell into the water. My eighty-four-year-old friend Bob rowed backwards toward it and retrieved it, this time more carefully, and carried it to land. Bob rowed backwards because he knows about pain. His mother died when he was eleven, and twelve years ago he lost a son.

Back in Cambridge and back to work.

I am sitting with a woman sobbing about having no one, being alone, saying when is it going to be my turn. She believes that somewhere it is written that life gets easier as one grows older. I don't interpret. I let her feel and tremble and shake with her pain. I know I can't fix her. I recognize a desire in myself to make her feel better, but I know too that whatever Band-Aid I could offer wouldn't really help. I am her therapist, not her friend or daughter or sister or mother. It's my job to help her tolerate the pain, and as I do that I feel my own pain. The underside of my skin also winces with its own coldness. I too wonder when it will be my turn to have some pleasure, some security, some happiness instead of just the chores and messy desks. Why is there no one for me who notices when I am desperate? At least for my client I am here watching, observing, shaking with her, holding back tears, knowing that she's wrestling with her panic and emptiness.

While waiting in the standby line for cars in Woods Hole at
5 p.m., I realize that it's Anatole's birthday. Seventy-two years
ago on this day in a bedroom of a house in the French Quarter of
New Orleans Anatole began his life. A small being struggling for
breath and life, the first son of a street-proud father. As our son
was being born on July 26, twenty-eight years ago, Anatole said
to me, "I love you." Did Anatole's father say these words to his
wife as Anatole was being born? I hope that if it was not said, the
feeling was there. By Anatole's report, his parents in later years
became rigid with each other. I wonder if July 16, 1920, was a
sunny day. Today began with moisture and clouds but now there
is a clear blue sky and a large lonely sun.

Three years ago the illness was a rumor. Two years ago Anatole was drugged with painkillers and unable to sit through his
own birthday party. He could sit in a chair for hors d'oeuvres
and the presents, but he had to retreat to our bed and the mercy
of unconsciousness for dinner. Will I always remember these
summer scenes of his final months of life so vividly—the desperation, mine and our friends', to keep him intact, functioning,
to keep him himself? We refused to let him slip. It made us
angry. We pinned the failure on him and not his illness. Our
great hurt had already begun. Anatole kept his private counsel.
He rarely let me see the pain. He withdrew with it. His books
and articles are very gallant, but there was the other side—the
muck and horror, the pull, the voyage to what we as humans
sense as nothingness. Certainly nothing physical remains. The
memory, the spirit of Anatole lingers, but gone is his hand to
hold, his shoulder to lean on.

Today I had one of my lost days. I couldn't function. It took
me three hours to straighten the kitchen, a job of, at most,
twenty minutes. All I could manage was a few phone calls. I
wandered from room to room, unable to sit or think about what
I should do because of the dead, without-breath feeling in my

body. I wandered as if there were no strings attaching me to anything at all. Sometimes I would sit at the piano and play seventeen measures of something. I let myself think about what I, we, had lost, think about the life we would be having now together. Anatole at the Vineyard, writing, going to the beach, and playing paddle ball, and I'd be going back and forth seeing clients, feeling somewhat sorry for myself but also glad to have some time to myself. We'd be planning a fall trip to France or England. We'd be trying to get our friends to go to a rock dance. Anatole would be jawing on the phone with Mike, a leg draped over the arm of a chair. He'd be criticizing my choice of books to read whenever I picked up a trashy biography. And I'd be knitting, not writing. Most important, we'd be happy in our imperfect, complaining, gossipy ways. We weren't always neat or orderly. We sometimes fought, but we were the best of friends.

I don't allow myself to think about these things often, because then I feel the hurt too precisely and then, the way I did today, I throw myself across our bed, pull into a fetal position, and cry and moan and sob, "Why," and "No," and "I want you, I want you to hold me," to an Anatole who can no longer touch me. Except that he did.

Before the operation I had become withdrawn, frightened about the hysterectomy, knowing that I would truly be going through it alone. Six days before the operation I woke up in the middle of the night and couldn't get back to sleep. This pattern had been developing for some weeks. I lay in bed and thought about how I would be dropped off at the Brigham at seven in the morning, left alone by Todd and Bliss because I did not want them to stay. I wouldn't want them to miss work on that day, because I would need them more when I came home. So there I would be alone, signing in, waiting, getting prepped. Thin, pale, tired.

These thoughts terrified me and I began to cry, quiet whimpering sobs as I lay huddled on my side, arms and knees to my chest, head down. Soft, wet, heaving cries finally turning to breaths. Then I felt an arm on my arm. A chest, a torso against my back. I breathed with the embrace. I turned and saw Anatole, and then turned back wanting not to see but rather just feel the drape of his arm, the solid mass of his chest against my back, his legs cupping mine. I needed him and he was there. Finally I turned my head and said, "Anatole, are you . . ." and then his face and body disassembled, evaporated, and he was gone. I turned back to my side profoundly comforted and fell asleep.

Reconnecting

When you drive down the final hill in Woods Hole and enter the parking lot of the Steamship Authority, where the ferries for Martha's Vineyard dock, as you roll down your window, you are asked, "Do you have a reservation?" If you don't, then you're motioned into the parking lot, where at the entry gate you say, "Standby," and an attendant puts a slip of green paper underneath your windshield wiper and directs you to the end of a line of parked cars. The green paper says:

STAND BY
Parking Lot Use Only
Not Good For Passage

Whenever I can't get a reservation on or off island ahead of time, I say to the steamship employee that it's okay because I'm probably the only person who doesn't mind waiting in the standby line. I'm relieved when I have no reservation, because then there is no deadline, no rush. I get to Woods Hole or to Vineyard Haven, depending on the direction of travel, when I can, and then I know I will wait.

You are asked not to leave your car for more than a half hour at a time because the lines get rotated to make additional space after each boat leaves with its segment of waiting cars. I stay in the car with my animals, two dogs and a cat. My life pulls me in too many directions. There is always a phone call to make, clothes to be transferred from the washer to the dryer, a search for the missing letter that needs to be answered. All these details pull me away from myself. In the standby line, sitting behind the wheel of my car, there are no interruptions, no thoughts of "better do this now." I don't turn on the radio. I sit quietly and wait as pieces of myself return to me and then I reach for pencil and paper, any paper will do, and I begin to write about my thoughts.

I look down at my hand scrawling words on paper, words not forced or asked for, words that just happen. The words form lines and then paragraphs, sometimes pages. Lead-gray lines on yellow paper that when I squint my eyes look like the hieroglyphics I'd seen as a child in the Egyptian wing of the Metropolitan Museum in New York.

I've had a tough week. I was sick last weekend with a high fever and shaking chills. It turned out to be Lyme disease, and now I'm on amoxicillin. My anger at one more setback—this on top of fleas in the Vineyard house—has been boundless. I am so furious at the current impulse to ascribe positive attributes to difficulties, illness, hard times. Why does there need to be a point to something, a lesson to learn, a gift to gain? Why isn't it enough to just keep going, to keep breathing, to not give up? Why is it not all right to give up? There should be more permission to collapse.

Twenty-some years ago I first saw Paul Taylor's *Esplanade,* set to Bach violin concertos. Dancers rush in, jump into the air, but they don't land. They fall. Fall on the floor, like a small child who hasn't yet learned that he has to protect himself from gravity. The fun, the daring of landing in a heap. The exuberance of simply giving in to weight. The thump, thud, noise of allowing yourself to drop and sprawl. There was one dancer in particular, a large-boned woman, who seemed to be able to intensify her weight as she crashed to the stage floor. The image of her falls is clear to me still. The exhilaration is there in my memory, with its defiance of the instinct to protect oneself by tensing up or doing a sleight of hand like rolling to reduce the impact. The total giving in to the consequences of being in the air. The crash that one can come out of so it's possible to do it all over again. The fall from grace. I remember this as I permit myself to give in, give up, fall down.

A man took me out to dinner, someone I had had a nodding acquaintance with. This was my first formal date since I was twenty-three. He came to pick me up. He opened the car door. He paid for dinner. We took a walk and a drive after. We talked in the car before he walked me to the door. I called the next morning to thank him. A few days later we met again to talk, tell stories, ask questions. I am happy and, perhaps, smitten. There is pleasure and aliveness in this adolescent feeling, but there is also the cautioning voice of some internalized regulator who says fine, go with the flow, this swirling current of infatuation, but don't lose your focus or work, or self. This man is a challenge. He's unreliable, but I must not make him into something in my mind that he is not. If I see him again, I must let him emerge from himself or withdraw back into himself, whatever he chooses. I need to be balanced with this, and yet my gulping, overboard self wants to inhale, consume, have him inside my skin, while the wiser part of me knows that it is better to remain separate, distinct, respect his life, his priorities, his agenda, and begin to get to know him and let him get to know me, if he chooses to. But being rational is not what I'm about.

What is this thing in me that wants to cut loose, fall off the edge? Is it like getting drunk? And so what if it is? Throwing myself at this man is not pouring alcohol down my throat, but then that behavior is not what I'd be most proud of the next day or morning after. I want to behave in a way that enhances and enlarges my life and self or what's the point. Better to stick with the fantasy.

Being interested in someone, having a light in my eye again for a man, has brought me back to the mainstream. There have been wonderful weekend days on the Vineyard. Lunches with friends, sailing on Menemsha Pond, being part once again of the summer festivities. In between I wait for phone calls. I know I am obsessed with this man.

But let me try to get beneath all this for a moment. I sense that what I'm really crying out for is just human contact, wanting a person to want me. But, listen, I do have a right to this wanting to be next to a man, to be holding hands and hip to hip with a strong irrational male presence who grabs my waist and winks at me from a distance. It is natural that I should desire these things and lose my balance in their presence.

I'm telling friends that I've met a man. Some are urging caution, but my rodeo friend, Barbara from Utah, says go for it. She told me to crawl on his bones and sing over his face. That's cowboy language for making love. This phrase leads me not to my new friend but instead back to Anatole. I realize that these past twenty-three months I have been crawling in his bones, and the writing, this new voice in me, could be said to be singing over his face.

The postures of grief. I hadn't thought about that before. A pulled-in, knees-to-arms, belly-and-forehead-near-the-floor way of moving seems right, the heaviness of grief making it impossible to balance upright for any length of time. Moving forward, inching along with grabbing knuckles and bloody knees, the terrain of grief is layered with the memories of illness, the pain, the fear, the dank holes of loss, of what could have been had there been no cancer, no death.

There is also a blindness with the crawling. Lights out, darkness, no coordinates to fix on, no landmarks on the horizon, no seeing into the future, because all that's known is the dense vapor of sticky tears and leaden weight as I carry my dead husband inside me.

The poet Galway Kinnell has a poem about tramping in the woods and coming upon a dead bear and crawling into his furry, blood-soaked, wet, torn carcass coat and trudging on with some kind of birth, death, birth process going on. I've heard him read this poem. I knew at the time that as I listened I was not hearing the narrative or structure or words of the poem. Instead his voice took me below the sense of the words into the more abstract meaning of sound and sensation, which was the transmogrification of man to beast to man. Crawling into the skin of the bear and heaving oneself forward through the forest, hearing this ten years ago and getting not the sense but the essence of the poem through the timbre of the poet's voice, this now seems like a presentiment, a preview of a coming attraction. On that warm summer night in the Katharine Cornell Theatre in Vineyard Haven in 1982 my tissue and cells knew and heard the message about crawling into the bones of someone else. Crawling into the bones of my dead husband, my last prolonged, protracted act of love with Anatole.

Paradoxically we, Anatole and I, have become more intimate in death than we ever were in life. And this is saying a lot, for we were very close in our marriage, even though we gave each other room. Anatole would spend one night a week in New York, and he once went to Vermont to write for four weeks, but other than that we were rarely separated. For many years he worked at home, so there was a lot of contact with meals together, walks together. But now I am his editor, the keeper of his light, and I have internalized him so I can do these things as he would have me do them with the sinew that remains, the strength, his strength that holds on and holds me together.

The ferry is docking. There is no one waiting for me. No face scanning the crowd, but I don't mind. I'm alone but I'm beginning to stand tall and feel sunlight on my hair. I'm curious about my future, for I've learned to sing and I've begun to dance again. The important thing today is that I do have the ability to be happy whether a relationship with this other man happens or not. I will be seeing him tonight.

There is some sadness after spending time with my new friend. In the bright light of day I wonder what my feelings for him are. The attraction, the melting tenderness for him yesterday, I know to keep these reactions in the context of the tremendous swings I've experienced. This summer, beginning as it did with the operation, was a time of anguish and withdrawal for me, so that a rush into strong feelings for this man may be a boomerang response arcing away from all the pain. He's a troublesome choice. I remind myself to be honest and cautious with him and to continue to work on the problems in my own life.

Driving down to Woods Hole this morning, sailing along Route 3, listening to Eric Clapton and the Indigo Girls, I felt clear and blessed, blood running swift and easily in my veins. I've earned these feelings; they have been wrought out of the effort, the patience, the commitment to life and to my marriage. With Anatole and all the problems in our marriage, I had finally learned to throw away the scorecard. I came to know and feel the great love I had for him, and when he died I stayed with the deep grief until I became sick myself. Until I, shaking and terrified of my own cancer, muttered and pleaded to myself and to Anatole and to God that no, I didn't want to die, I wanted to live.

There are so many gifts in my life. I am grateful for how my friends and I nudge one another's souls. Like cats we rub our necks and cheeks against one another.

Tonight I took off my wedding ring, the gold band from Georg Jensen that we bought our second year of marriage because the first gold band looked like a curtain ring. It had been on the third finger of my left hand for thirty-one years. Tonight is the second anniversary of the last night I saw Anatole alive. The Weismans were here with the Kintslingers, the Grand-Jeans, and Nancy Cetlin. A congenial group, all close friends. I clinked my knife against my glass and began to talk about Anatole's death, about Suzy and Hugh spending their twenty-ninth wedding anniversary with us. I said it was time for me to remove my ring. I put it on the silver chain with the other talismans, the dog, the heart, the hexagon, that I wear around my neck.

Two years ago I went to sleep at twelve-thirty and was woken by a phone call at six-thirty to hear that Anatole had died. I waited a half hour to tell Bliss, thinking, Let her have another half hour in her life where she has a father. If I could conjure Anatole back, place him alive and breathing next to me, I would, even with all his faults, because he was my husband, and for better or for worse I loved him. But I can't, so instead I have decided that I want to be happy. I want love and tenderness and desire and tension in my life. But for now on this second anniversary I remain quiet and alone. The guests have left and the kitchen has been cleaned up.

My new friend has not called. His answering service annoyingly says, "Have no idea where he is." So instead of feeling cut off, adrift, I think about writing him a letter. Perhaps my age, my directness, my presence are a turnoff for him. If this is true, that's all right, because I am who I am. I feel okay about myself. In fact I feel good. There are other men who will find me attractive. And at this point, as I'm imagining this letter while making myself toast and tea in the kitchen, the light above the sink flashes off and on. I stop and say, "Anatole, you silly man, what are you trying to tell me, that you say bravo to my sharp sense of self?" I don't write the letter. The thought of it is enough.

A few days later I read the chapter "Homing: Returning to Oneself" in *Women Who Run with the Wolves*. Estes tells the story of a seal woman who has shed her sealskin to live on land with a human man and birth and raise a child. By the time the child has grown to be a boy, the seal woman has become dried, weakened, blind. She needs her sealskin, her soulskin, so she can return to the sea, her home where her soul self will be restored by the ease of moving through water, being buoyant in water, where her eyes made moist once again by the salty sea will pierce the shadowed depths with brightness. For the seal woman, the sea is the home that she so desperately needs to return to. For the rest of us, "Home," Estes writes, "is where a thought or feeling can be sustained instead of being interrupted or torn away from us because something else is demanding our time and attention." It is where ideas, creativity, and songs are birthed. Estes admits that "it is hard to go, really, really hard to cede, to hand over whatever we've been so busy with and just leave," to return home. Perhaps my not dealing with certain areas of my life, like housework and mail, is a way of ceding or leaving.

Where is my soul home? Well, I do have it here in the Vineyard. I get a whiff of it on standby line. When I write, I'm home with myself. When I dance. When I do therapy, garden, stencil. All this gives me joy. Here on Abel's Hill thoughts surface. The air is soft.

This morning in ballet class Igor was playing great music during the frappés. Igor is a classically trained pianist who takes off from the written score with his own commentaries on Chopin, Tchaikovsky, Mozart, and Beethoven. The melodic line was emotive, charged, full, and sparkling, and it got me and my legs and feet into a place they don't often get.

Frappés always remind me of Edward Caton, a ballet teacher at the Joffrey Studio in the early sixties who had danced with Pavlova in Russia. Pants pulled high on his waist, his shoes worn down on the outside of his heels, he would demonstrate with his hands the timing and energy of single and double frappés—"in, in . . . out!"—with a shade of emphasis on the second "in" and then the "out" arriving a hair's breadth before its time, so that the speed of the foot from ankle to the extended dégagé was very fast, followed by the brief stillness of the dégagé. With frappés I always have the sense of some ideal place to be, because of their preciseness and sharpness. The delineation is exact. When I find it and am there with the strength and energy of the movement, it is wonderful. Today that happened. Marcus noticed. And either before or after he noticed, I had this thought: that dying in the middle of a sharply executed frappé wouldn't be so bad. It might in fact be rather nice. Certainly a clear transition—a quick death.

That is not how Anatole died. Instead there was a slow leaking of his animation, his ability to move. A creeping paralysis crawled over and in and through his body, as his electrolytes and fluids went astray. Anatole would have preferred, as he had written in his notes, a leap into death, to cut ties with this life at the height of a volleyball spike, to jump up at the net, hand slamming the ball, and then the spirit keeps soaring like a rocket blastoff, while the body collapses on the sand, on a cloudless day with dune grass and ocean as backdrop. Brook's death was better, the heart attack while washing a car. He had the Ford dealership in Manchester and had sold six cars that day.

I hate what happened to Anatole, the pain, the torture. I remember him in the first room at Dana Farber, being barely able to walk over to the chair by the window, telling the doctor about his once beautiful feet that were now swollen and unrecognizable. The doctors, the nurses, they've all seen this before. They knew, they were familiar with the progression. We weren't. Our naïveté kept us believing that there could be a reversal, a restoration, a return to normal. I suppose the doctors and nurses also knew that it was important for us not to know what lay ahead, the horror of dying from cancer.

I remember one night hearing the cries of a man at the end of the hall whose physical pain was not covered by the pills and IV drips. He shouted, "Help me. Owww! I can't stand this. No!" I don't think anyone was with him. He died a few days later.

After an intense week of work, I'm unwinding in Chilmark, letting the leaves go where they will and deciding that I really don't have to wash the windows. The ashen-gray weather this October weekend has been oddly warm and comforting. Work has picked up at the two clinics where I am on staff. On Thursdays I sometimes can have as many as ten clients scheduled back-to-back. Thank goodness there is usually one cancellation. Before these days I feel as though I am preparing for a marathon.

Returning to Cambridge early Tuesday morning, I slowly drive down Abel's Hill with a Mozart piano concerto filling the car, my eyes drawn to the soft colors and heather blends of the up-island foliage and the distant low, gray linear clouds of early morning stretched across Chilmark Pond and the ocean. These scenes and views of the Vineyard do not stay outside me. Like the music they drift in and to me. They touch my skin, pass through its pores, and sink into my soul. The Vineyard at these times becomes my lover. With lingering looks my gaze turns into longing as I drive down to Vineyard Haven to catch the ferry to go off island for four days and three nights. In the summer the mixture of bay and oak and pine and wild hydrangea is only a dense tangle of green, but now in the fall the true personalities of these plants emerge. As if by a communal decision, they have agreed not to show their colors and state their name until the summer population leaves. These scruffy plants are true islanders. Proud of their heritage, private in their manners, wise in their behavior, they emerge only when the island has been returned to itself, when the traffic and busyness of summer have gone.

As I breathe in these Vineyard scenes, I wonder if the Vineyard is sensing me, yearning for me. Are these muted colors, bathed in a soft light, a form of courtship drama, the landscape revealing itself in order to draw me close, tug on my soul, so that I will begin the transition to someone who lives on the island? Am I beginning to be caught up in this transition from ordinary person to island resident? Do I have a choice in the matter or am I chosen? I know that this love, this passion is real, as real as the rise and fall of my breath, which follows the flow of the waves of Vineyard Sound that lap against the hull of the ferry.

New Directions

odd loses his car today. He had leased a Ford Thunderbird when he was doing well selling alarm systems in the Boston area, but the economic slump of 1990 has severely cut back the market and his sales, and now he can't make the payments. Like a bankruptcy, this will destroy his credit. It pains me that I can't pick up the payments for him, but they are $400 a month and that's not possible to do.

This morning I am realizing how angry I am and that I have not known it. Cleaning the living room, I see that Belle has peed on the large wing chair with the Belgian linen floral slipcover. I lose my temper with her, telling her that she's an impossible cat. The bad mood also has to do with having had some good times with this new man who has now disappeared. I long for a distraction. Meanwhile I call Marcus and tell him about my problems. I hang up knowing I've just talked about the surface, not the turmoil underneath.

Here I am at age fifty-four, postmenopausal, no uterus, on hormones, and I'm crazed by the desire to jump, leap, leave the mess of my life, burst through, break apart all assumptions about age and decorum. I want to streak across the sky, throw myself at the heavens, fall and tumble down a canyon, dive into deep waters, have dirt, sand, mud cling to my skin, wedge under my fingernails, cake in my ears, mat down my hair. I want to feel more, see more, do more, move more, go to forbidden places. I want some compensation for all my losses, for all the shit that's been shoved in my face, forced into my heart. This is what I wanted to say to Marcus.

I have a fury beyond tears because Anatole died, because Brook died, because Jassy died. As one of my psychotherapy clients says, "I'm owed something for this," but she doesn't know how to demand payment. She expects good things will happen. Not so. They don't just happen. You have to go out and grasp and reach, take and use, climb and crawl and, yes, even grovel. Drop the mooring, sail the boat no matter what the weather. Don't fear the wind. My soul is screaming for solace, for passion, for love, for a grand waltz whose dipping and turning movements will carry me, transport me to a place of bliss, or ease, to the land of the Sugar Plum Fairy, where all is sweet and right and enchanted and beautiful. But then I would miss the rough texture of my current life, the gravelly way it grates and scratches, giving me workman's hands and muscles.

I can see now that the contretemps with the unavailable man was a passionate and yearning wish because he had flashing eyes and a wicked smile and strong legs and back, because there was a chemistry that had to do with the unavailability, the unpredictable quality, some part of me being stuck in an unresolved adolescence. As Sherry quoted the Beckett phrase to me some months ago, "I can't go on. I go on."

Back on my favorite ferry going to Vineyard Haven. The *Islander* was launched the year I first came to the Vineyard, in

1954. The engines shudder and rumble. Years of scraping and repainting have built up a gesso-like surface on her bulkheads and interior walls. This is the vessel in the Steamship fleet that can make port when the others can't, for she has a wheelhouse both stern and aft so she doesn't need to turn to dock. This helps in bad weather. Her shape, her simple lines and deck plan are emblematic of the Vineyard for me.

For the most part there are fewer thoughts about the man who stopped calling. The leaden sky of this November day tells me to prepare for winter, to finish the outdoor chores, come inside and sit near the stove.

This weekend I hung out with some Vineyard friends, people who had grown up on the island. I was aware that I was feeling sad and alone, distant from people. While I was with them there was a part of myself that was telling me that if I had really connected with the unavailable man, then these friends, for they are also his friends, would be my new context, and some niggly voice inside was meanly thinking that this would make a limited, shrunken-down life. No, that's wrong. I'm just trying to rationalize why the departed man is not for me instead of admitting the loss, the ripping away of arms, hands, eyes, smiles, all those things that enchanted me. I want to remain his friend. And what if this is just the first chapter? Perhaps we will get together again. He will call. The other demands and interests of his life will release him. We will reconnect.

Wait. There is something familiar here, a parallel with not accepting Anatole's impending death in his last few months. There he was, losing weight, losing energy, suffering from increasing pain, and I insisted on believing that there could be a cure. Insisted on believing that he would live, that the badness would go away, that our special connection would persevere. So now with the unavailable man I am doing the same thing. A part of me is not willing to see his pulling away, the turn of his back, his shift of interest. I talk about taking pride in my rational stability and emotional maturity, but what about this stubbornness, this need to believe, the grasp that does not let go?

I shouldn't have sent the letter and the excerpt from Elizabeth Hardwick's *Sleepless Nights* about the small boy throwing objects out a window. The disappearing man had told me that as a child he once threw a television set out a window. In a way I've been thrown out a window. I crowded him, made him claustrophobic so he had to disappear, pull away, rise as if in water to get some air.

I'm beginning to know that I want, absolutely want, to be with another man, but I'm scared that I won't be able to connect. My timing will be wrong. I'll miss the boat, or I'll sink it. I'll miss my chance, my salvation. I know that I can only be saved by myself, but I'm desperate for the holding, the contact of soft tissue, skin next to skin, pulse to pulse, breath to breath, the ease, the consolation of human warmth.

Last night a man I've recently met invited me to have dinner with him. Clearly he is interested, but am I? I don't know. He walks with small steps and that bothers me. Perhaps I should hum the refrain from Bach's Cantata no. 78, "We hasten with eager yet feeble footsteps." He is smart, attractive, sensitive, warm, and considerate, and appears strong. There seemed to be some noticeable current between us, but that is the way I am feeling about any man I'm around these days. I wonder about Marcus and myself. His neurotic unavailability attracts me, as do his wit and his sadness. I want to cradle and hold his sadness. In some way Marcus and I are soulmates. Two lone birds with wounded wings who can still fly. He is my teacher, and we are close friends. The intimacy already in place seems to stop us from becoming anything more.

Today I'm driving down to New York for two appointments. A shamanic session with River and then a meeting with a woman from the Mayo Clinic in Rochester, Minnesota. Mary Adams Martin is in charge of the annual presentation of issues pertinent to medical practice, which are presented in a theatrical form.

This year the topic is the doctor-patient relationship, and Anatole's book, *Intoxicated by My Illness,* is being considered as a text for a dramatic monologue.

In the car I continue to think about the men in my life and the men that are not in my life, and as I do this, I realize once again that I need to focus on myself, my work, and supporting Todd through his tough times. This bouncing off walls, not knowing my feelings, keeps me spinning. I need a guide.

As I wait for her on East Thirty-eighth street, I remember that River is always late. Thoughts come again about my need, my mood for romance. Like all the hours at Loehmann's that I've spent trying on clothes, I want to try these men on for size. See what fits, what makes me feel good, look good, sound good, who brings out the me that is me or the me of my fantasies or the me that I could become, who heightens my color.

After we have lunch at a Thai restaurant on Third Avenue, River gives me a simultaneous acupuncture and spirit animal session.

First, she feels my pulses. My pancreas has improved, which means the ability to transform food into Chi energy is better. My left pulse is good, stronger than before. I don't know what that means. My liver still needs strengthening. She traces a figure-eight pattern on my abdomen to regulate my hormones. I had told her about the Premarin I was taking to help with sleep and other symptoms of menopause. River recommends that I discontinue the hormones, because of the risk of breast and ovarian cancer.

She inserts the first needle in my right inside forearm. There is discomfort and warmth. More needles are placed in my left forearm and the inner sides of both insteps and one or two in my belly. The needles sting as they go in. River tells me how to find my power animals. She speaks about going down into an opening, a hole, down into the earth. From there I am to travel along a dark subterranean corridor and emerge in a different landscape. She says I may see animals underground. When I come up, and it could be into a desert or a jungle, a high or low place, I am to notice any animals that are present. I might see one, more than one. I follow her instructions and I come out onto a flat plain. The only animal I see is a toad. He is warty and has a big flap, like a cap with a visor, on his head. I think about other animals but I see only the toad.

After these verbal instructions the real journey begins, with River drumming a medium steady beat. She tells me to go to a high place. She sees me being lifted up into the air on a kite, a balloon, a waft of smoke, so as to have a larger range of vision to search for my animals. I choose in my imagination to walk up the hill behind our Vineyard house to the Indian graveyard deep in the woods, and there I meet some deer, lady deer with no antlers. Together, I and the deer fly up into the air, first to Noman's to look for more animals and then to the Elizabeth Islands, where we find a quiet bear beginning to hibernate, a black-brown bear. Together the deer, two or three of them, the bear, and I go off to search for a panda. We travel so far west that we find ourselves in northern Japan. There on an island in a cold hideaway is a panda, but when I see this bear, I know that he is not my power animal, nor is the crescent-moon bear that we next meet. The plain dark-brown bear who is sluggish is the bear meant for me. My bear is hazy for me on this trip, which means I have to spend more time with him. River had said earlier that it is important that on these searching trips we return on the same path that we journeyed on going outward; otherwise we cause a loop and become shackled by awkward junk. Taking her word for it, I retrace my steps. River, in her mind, had accompanied me with her power animal, wolf. Taking a taxi over to the West Side to meet with Mary Adams Martin, I see a restaurant called The Wicked Wolf.

Mary is a beautiful, elegant, petite seventy-four-year-old woman who suggests that Jason Robards could do dramatized readings of Anatole's illness book. He is her friend of many years and has performed in these Mayo events before. We agree that work and ourselves are the wellsprings of our lives. Her husband had died suddenly when she was fifty, the day after their son's marriage. We decide to do a collaboration using Anatole's words. Isaiah Sheffer, who directs Symphony Space in New York, will extrapolate a monologue from the chapter "The Patient Examines the Doctor." The production is scheduled for early March of next year.

Late November now and I'm keeping the water on in the Vineyard until December first. This is a risk, but it does take longer for the pipes to freeze in the fall than in the spring. There are fewer weekend people on the Vineyard, and the island is turning back to itself. Cars are scarce on the road. When they pass each other drivers wave, for everyone knows everyone now. Leaving Woods Hole, the ferry pulls away from the dock, definite in its course, heading for its other port, guided by the red bell buoys. Thinking less these days about men, I also am heading back to my other port, which is myself, my work, my life, the fullness and challenges that are there. The victories and accomplishments that await will truly be mine, truly feed me, securely support me.

As I spend these long weekends in Chilmark in an uninsulated house with only the woodstove for warmth, the weather gets colder, last night down to the high twenties. I find that I am comfortable in the cold. Only the main room, I call it the keeping room, as in an eighteenth-century house, the room where the cooking, living, reading, and mending was done, only this room where the stove sits is warm. Upstairs the living room and my bedroom and bathroom are chilly, about 40 degrees, and yet I am coming to like the cold air on my face and bare skin when I change clothes or take a bath. My complexion is improving.

Years ago when I was crossing the Atlantic with my mother on the MS *Oslofjord,* bound for Norway, those last few days before her death, on that ship there was a Norwegian girl returning home to Oslo from Smith. She was beautiful in a direct, uncomplicated Scandinavian way. Clear features and shoulder-length brown hair. She was aloof and not very friendly, or perhaps I saw her that way because I was shy and had been at Mt. Holyoke, which I thought of as a school for women who were mousy compared with their Northampton sisters. Sometimes we would meet on the open deck of this boat sailing the North Atlantic in early June. There might have been sun, but it was a chilled sun and the wind was cold. I would shiver self-consciously, sure that the rattle of my bones and teeth was audible, while this young woman was serene and composed in the cool air—a Nordic goddess who was unruffled, who could sail the cold northern waters and see far, know all, not be distracted by thin skin, goose bumps, and irregular spasmodic shakes. Now as I live with the falling temperatures of late fall, as I putter in cold rooms, bring in wood, walk the dogs on the beach, I no longer shiver. The cold air has become my friend, my element, the climate that encourages me to thrive. The exterior cold has enabled me to develop warmth from within. It is bringing color to my face and alertness to every cell in my body.

After class today, walking back to the car, I was thinking about the card Christopher Davis had sent, which said, "It is knowing this kind of thing and I think this kind of thing only, that makes art worth doing." A few weeks ago, browsing the books in Anatole's study, I had noticed that Anatole had written his name in the flyleaf of Davis's *A Peep into the Twentieth Century,* which is something that he never did. Favorite books were always being passed on to friends with no name in the flyleaf as a reminder of who was the lender. This book, one of his favorites, was an exception. It was often lent, but Anatole must have felt particularly concerned about its being returned. I had dropped the author a note telling him this.

His small card, his acknowledgment of my note, is a reminder to me of why I continue to dance. That art is worth doing because of these small but true responses, like the feedback I've received over the years from some of my dance students. These personal acknowledgments provide the embers that feed the larger effort that is the work, the daily discipline and the daily doing. This sense of the small response moving mountains or the fabric of one's life is akin to the basic principle of Feldenkrais work. The small adjustment affects the whole. And then I realized how small events in my day can cause a waterfall of associations and ideas. When I was only thinking about my unavailable friend, this hadn't been happening. I'd lost myself, my imaginative friction. This is the price I'd paid for the high, the joy, and the pleasure of his company, but the rush of a whirling attraction does not satisfy the me that is emerging, the me that thrills in dance classes, the me that writes, the me that helps people. If I am to have a relationship with a man, perhaps it will be one where the nuances are finer, more discrete, where the passion moves me in a more diminutive way, but where the whole effect reaches further into how I move, how I conduct my life, how I live.

> *When from our better selves we have too long*
> *Been parted by the hurrying world, and droop,*
> *Sick of its business, of its pleasures tired,*
> *How gracious, how benign, is Solitude.*
> —Wordsworth

Cut out from a Celestial Seasonings package and now on the side of the red refrigerator in the keeping room.

Alone tonight, polished some brass but mainly sat and knit and watched the fire while the radio was tuned to *Classical Haven* on WMVY, the local Vineyard station. Listening to Copland's *Rodeo* and Stravinsky's *Dumbarton Oaks*, I thought about what this music had meant to me when I first became familiar with it living alone in New York City and studying modern dance in 1959, the year after my parents and Ben died. The rhythms, the tonality, the style were different from the more predictable music of my parents' record collection and the choral music I had sung in high school. This differentness paralleled the alien quality of my life in New York, after I suddenly lost my father, my mother, and between those two deaths my boyfriend, Ben, who died in a car accident. Three people to whom I was closest—all gone in nine months, October, December, and then June.

As I hear the music tonight, the haunting harmonies of Stravinsky in 6/8 and 7/8 time, I again see the main studio of the Graham School and remember the strangeness of the long combinations we did across the floor, coming diagonally from the corner. At that time I believed that these movement phrases held some knowledge about life that was not yet accessible to me. I had been tossed or perhaps abandoned to a different world, a more abstract world by these deaths. I would go see the Graham Company perform and not understand what they were doing, except to know that there was good technique and fine energy and that this strange resonant music spoke of distant lands and of missions and tasks not yet conceived.

Then, thirty years later, I saw another performance of the Graham Company. This time in Boston. A Saturday matinee with a husband ill with cancer. Now I could understand everything on stage. In *Acts of Light* I saw that this dance was about Martha's struggle between love and passion for a man, and love and passion for her art. It was all so clear. She wanted romance, but she wanted her art more, so she did her art, and she did her art relentlessly, and she gave birth. She produced light and joy and pleasure. The dance opens with the company doing the floor work from class. These are dancers sharing the most private of secrets in a dancer's life: that it is pure bodily pleasure to enter a studio and warm up the instrument of their art, bending and stretching, contracting and releasing, reaching and pulling back, curving through space, celebrating one's own weight, one's presence, one's most immediate experience of self, bringing to a perfect pitch the cells and sinews of one's body. Martha developed a technique of moving and warming up the body that invited passion, passion fired by the spark of finding unknown parts of one's self. She would say in class, "There is so little time to be born in a moment." We all gave birth to our selves, our dancing selves, and the birth was totally physical, not intellectual or emotional. Certainly not the latter, for many of us were lost souls in some sense.

At the end of the performance in Boston, Martha, ninety years plus, appeared onstage, propped up by her dancers, standing there in the long column of an iridescent Halston sheath. I began crying. I couldn't stop. I cried shaking sobs as I walked up the aisle at my husband's side. I cried all the way to our car two blocks away. Anatole never said anything. Perhaps he thought I was crying about his illness. I wasn't. I was crying about my not dancing, about what still needed to be born in me, about how Martha was still there in my life, about what her work had revealed to me, in me, as I saw it over the years and came to understand her choreography through the lens of my own experience. I sobbed because I knew what it was to do those deep contractions and sudden swirling long strikes and releases and crawling on the floor as if one were suspended in the firmament of heaven, crawling as if one were a constellation of stars, shards of light shifting and changing but the shape never lost and the name always Greek, Cassandra, Ariadne, Clytemnestra. There was nothing petty or small or ordinary about the Graham work. There was always grandeur, statements, affirmation, dedication, and light that turned up the volume of aliveness. Walking down Tremont Street to the car, I wanted this back for myself and for my husband, for he was also a dancer, but he'd never stopped shining. His words were his light, his movement, his affirmation. And yes, I suppose, I was crying for him, for the slow leak his illness was causing that was draining away his life.

Standing Still

December 5, my mother's birthday. She would have been ninety-six today.

I was sailing *Swallow* this summer with no anchor. That seems perfectly reasonable to me, for I have no anchor, no solid weighty object that will in a storm hold me fast. When I cry I get swept away in the current of my own grief. If friends ever read this they will say, Why didn't you tell me? I care about you. But the facts are that I believe I have told them about the pain or perhaps I only begin to tell them about the pain and then stop. They want to fix, and that makes my isolation worse.

Reading *Care of the Soul,* by Thomas Moore, I underline "Observance means listening and looking at what is being revealed in the suffering. . . . An intent to heal can get in the way of seeing. . . . By doing less, more is accomplished. . . . Feel the drama more intensely and imagine it more precisely." I'm not sure this is good advice.

December 12 is my birthday. It depresses me that I am turning fifty-five. Marcus calls and tells me not to feel bad, that being fifty-five only means that I've finally reached the speed limit. Why that makes me feel better, I don't know, but it does.

To celebrate I decide to befriend my desk. I sit on the swiveling, cushioned desk chair and lean over the blue blotter and wade through the papers. Sitting at my desk is a way of being with myself that's been hard to do since Anatole died. I've been too frantic, too reactive, too frightened to sit down and be patient and calm. As a child I sometimes yelled, "I can't. I won't." Who was forcing me? I have no idea. There were no childhood traumas, only directive parents and a willful child. The bad stuff came later in my life. Now I will tell myself, "I can. I will."

Why do I write these words? I am obsessed with myself when I write. My fear is that my words take me to a place that distances me from others. I become too specific, perhaps too present. In a certain way even with Anatole I was often alone, kept apart from him by his design, his neurosis. Perhaps it's easier now to be truly alone. I don't even want to sleep with the animals anymore.

I had a dream a few weeks ago. I knew I should have written it down at the time but I didn't. Perhaps I wanted to ignore the sense of the dream, not face its experience. What I remember is this.

I was making love to a man similar to Anatole, if not Anatole. I had clothes on, layers like long johns, piecemeal tights and leotards. We moved to an inside room and began caressing again. I said, "Wait a minute," and drew back to take off all my clothes and then drew near again. At this point the man pulled back, saying he couldn't continue. We left the bedroom and walked away through a parking lot and down a hill. I was so angry that I wouldn't speak to the man even though he tried to talk to me. My anger had the strength of fury and this was remarkable to me, that I had so much rage, so much that I refused to speak to him. He had wanted me and was caressing me, and I trusted his gestures and his behavior to the point where I disrobed entirely. I unclothed not only my body, but also my feelings, and then at this point, not earlier, my nakedness, a place where I was defenseless, put this man off. My presence shut him off, caused him to turn away. Clearly, this is a fear I have with men and with people. Their rejection if I reveal myself.

What is wrong with me? Why the pressure, the work, the loss upon loss? But to balance this all, why the dancing? Why do I even care about being happy?

Last night, I saw Paula Josa-Jones's brilliant solo *The Messenger*. Her company rehearses at the Green Street Studio, where Marcus teaches. In her dance, Paula caught the physicality of isolation and fear with their need to hide within, coupled with uncontrollable leaks and outbursts. She presented herself as half man and half woman. The repression and confinement of the male frock coat and hat and glasses were followed by a weighty, hip-slugging walk of a bearded prostitute leering at the audience, daring in the eyes. When Anatole's oldest friend, Milton Klonsky, died, his last word was *debauchery*. Paula danced that and the tragedy of that, the aloneness of it and the crippledness of it. Having seen this dance, I realize that my grief feels almost sexual. It transports me and carries me, but there is no pleasure, only pain.

Spent the weekend working on another book of Anatole's. The solitude feels good. My being craves this just as my body needs water and food. When I'm caught up in my weekly schedule I forget how badly I want this. I forget how there is something that begins to settle in me when I am alone. The sensation is of an unhinging and shedding of the hard, brittle scales that keep my façade intact, so that once again I am soft and breathing is easier.

Yet what do I come back to when I'm alone? More death. I am working on Anatole's Greenwich Village memoirs and stories, and I am there with Anatole as his father is dying, as Anatole is struggling to live. His words are about moving, stillness, dancing and death and sex, giving spontaneous birth to himself while he struggles with his roots, his parents, consoling himself with women as he loses his father.

Then Ann calls, one of the few people I can tolerate talking to when I'm alone, as she too knows and treasures aloneness, for she's a painter. She tells me about a dead pigeon she's found and is painting at her studio in Boston. In between painting sessions she places the bird on an outside windowsill to preserve it in the chill January air. She knows she is painting death. She sees it in the drab colors of the bird's feathers.

I tell her about Anatole's description of his father dying, hands sculpting the suffering. I wonder if the bird harks back to Ann's experience of nursing her father to his death two years ago. She says that perhaps the bird is preparing her for her mother's death or even her own.

Ann with her father and I with Anatole have stood at the bedside and watched and hovered and wiped the brow, held the hands, caressed the cheek of those we love as they die. The experience has been ground into our bones. Our structure, our carriage, our needs are different, and part of that difference is our need to be alone, to be silent, not to jabber or do busy work, but be quiet and wait.

Browsing through Wallace Stevens's *The Collected Poems,* I read a poem I had not noticed before: "Waving Adieu, Adieu, Adieu."

> *That would be waving and that would be crying,*
> *Crying and shouting and meaning farewell,*
> *Farewell in the eyes and farewell at the centre,*
> *Just to stand still without moving a hand.*

If I stand still, others will not see my hurt or pain because it is myself and only myself that takes care of my inner wreckage. That's my private business. I am learning how to do that.

My sister suggests I spend a few days in the sun and warm air. She lives just outside Naples, Florida. When I arrive, before driving to her home, we stop at an upscale resale shop for women's clothes that she has told me about. I find a brown wool pinstriped dress with a velvet collar from a Paris designer for $40. Shopping is something that we have a great deal of fun doing together. Her great-books group is reading *Intoxicated by My Illness*. They invite me to a meeting and we discuss Anatole's writing. My sister and I sit in an outdoor Jacuzzi late at night and talk about our father and the importance to him of doing what he felt to be right. Barbara is a doer, not an examiner, and these four days turn out to be a vacation from myself with the schedule of lunches, dinners, and meeting my brother-in-law and sister's friends.

Returning to Boston, while waiting on the ground in Raleigh, I noticed from my window seat on the airplane a cardboard box on a wooden pallet sliding out of the cargo bay onto a trolley, bound to the pallet with two blue metal bands. EXTREME CARE is written on the outside in the aqua Florida blue of Naples. A coffin, someone's final journey, noticed by a fifty-five-year-old woman, while chasing memories, connections to past and future. A young handsome olive-skinned boyish man says excuse me. He has the seat next to mine, a young Anatole. He pulls out a book. I can't see the title. The author is Mary Shelley. Do these details mean something or do I just note the poetry as it occurs, seeing the image, the metaphor, which like a gel in a stage light illuminates some corner of feeling, some shard of experience past, present, or future? The young man is reading *Frankenstein*.

Saw Marcus's First Night tape. His work has come to a new place, beyond the need to find a theme or subject. It's coming from its own source—the collaboration between Igor and himself and his work, his art and his classes. Another one of those walls where a door has opened. The wall being the evolution of his art.

The man who walks with small steps and I had brunch at Rebecca's on Charles Street after a walk through a frigid Boston Common seeing ice skaters on the ponds and identifying trees, watching a leaf on Beacon Hill ride the wind currents, refusing to fall, and finally nesting against a crosshatch of branches. Tomorrow he and I go to the Vineyard for the day. There is no water at the house, and it is too cold to stay there even with the woodstove. In these past two and a half years I have almost always been alone in the car, using the privacy to cry, to dream, to wander through the jumble of myself and then just stay with that. Arriving in Woods Hole, reaching for my notebook and a pencil and writing while I wait for the ferry, writing while I am on the ferry, struggling to put myself on paper, struggling to make sense of the continuing disorder of myself and my life. These are my rituals.

But tomorrow I will have company. There will be a man with me, a sensitive man who watches and listens when he's with me. What is it I am losing by having his company? What am I trading for the solace of his attention? Will I lose the meditations I have with myself? And if I do, is that really something that matters?

I've heard that Paula Josa-Jones will be doing a series of classes in authentic movement in a barn forty minutes west of Cambridge. Authentic movement is a process of improvisation that is done in silence and is witnessed by the other group members. Responses and reactions to what is seen in others and perceived in one's own dancing are about content and expression, not technique or agility. I have signed up for the eight sessions.

In the first class Paula talks about getting back to zero. She uses nouns with no modifiers. Back to zero in order to start or find her new solo. She goes from standing up to lying down to find something that is not being searched for, to find something the way life gives up gifts. As she moves she changes levels and her supports, going from her back to the side, then weight on a thigh and head, a forearm and foot. I see the distinctions between waking and sleeping. After the class, driving back to Cambridge, one of the class members tells me I move like an adolescent. Is that good or bad?

In the past few weeks I've been having spells of intermittent nausea. Whenever I am weak and unable to eat I remember how I was with Anatole, my lack of empathy, how I couldn't accept his statements of not feeling well. When he couldn't do something I would see this as resistance, a caving-in, a refusal to fight for his life. I was terrified by his need to rest. I mistrusted the lying still, being still, seeing it as a rehearsal for death.

Anatole was always so physically active in his life. He was a prime mover. He couldn't sit still. On a beach he was forever jumping up to play paddle ball, volleyball, throw a Frisbee. He could not, would not lie still under the summer sun. So when he began to lie still on our bed throughout the afternoon, the fear of his leaving me would begin to shrivel the edges of my being, like a piece of paper smoldering. To extinguish this burning I would insist that he get up, that we do something, sit and watch TV, a video, anything. When he couldn't do these things, then I would crawl into bed with him and rub his back, pretending to myself and saying to him that my hands had the power to heal, that the kneading and massaging of my palms and fingers as they caressed and rubbed his spine, his deltoid and trapezius muscles would make him well. I had to believe that I was powerful or I couldn't have gone on from day to day.

I've picked up a copy of Deepak Chopra's latest book, *Quantum Healing*. He writes about Chi, the vital life force.

"Increase the heat in the body. . . . Massage can cure. . . . Body has to move. . . . Movement is as important as eating and sleeping."

All these phrases jump out at me as I read along, like Burma Shave signs alongside flat Midwestern roads.

Paula said today that my improvisation was like origami with its deep folds. While I was dancing the barn door blew ajar. A blast of cold wind swirled around my feet. I swiftly closed it, saying, not yet. Then, I was in a duet and didn't realize it. We had been moving for forty-five minutes with silence and stillness, eyes closed.

There's always movement, glacial movement, change, even while one is still. Being aware of my feet, holding my left foot, feeling the instep, the sole, caressing my left sole, remembering Anatole trying to walk at Dana Farber, remembering how he walked across Mt. Auburn Street toward the hospital to his appointment for the cystoscopy. That was not lost to me. I remembered the story about his father, written in 1950, "What the Cystoscope Said." The narrator first senses his father's terminal illness when he sees him walking down the street wearing a neck brace. As I watched Anatole walk, seeing him swagger toward his destiny, I remember knowing then and fearing then that he would, I would, be robbed of the pleasure of that walk. His arms were swinging, not loosely but in a syncopated rhythm to match the slight hesitation in his walk that was really a dance.

A year and some months later at Dana Farber he looked down at his feet and saw them swollen and misshapen. He asked the doctor, What's happened to my feet? I used to have beautiful feet. With a nurse he took eight shuffling steps over to a chair by a window, and that was the last time he sat in a chair. He was moving toward his final stillness. To walk no more. To dance no more. To think no more.

Being still, moving with glacial slowness, allows thoughts to slowly surface and I know that as they happen they are grief's journey. Fifteen more minutes of moving, standing, walking, hands on hips feeling the strength and layers of fiber, tissue, the solid mass that supports and moves me, its density, the cohesiveness of my hips. Standing feels confining. Why so much standing up? The range of options feels limited, balancing on these two long limbs. Why all the shifts of weight from leg to leg and all the shapes and angles of bent knee, flexed foot, pointed toe? Because legs are expressive. They need to talk. They tell stories, reveal secrets. They can be funny, witty, serious. Legs can surprise. They can conceal. Legs are not only for standing. Legs talk even when they are quiet. Something is percolating. They're waiting to move, to explore, to carry me into my life. I open my eyes and look out the window and see the winter branches of trees and bushes, a few leaves tenaciously hanging on, refusing to fall. These legs, these branches that support and move me through the greenness of summer, the blaze of autumn, they are still now or appear to be. I am thinned out and porous. Only in Paula's class, in the stillness, do I feel motion. In the stillness, those hours on Thursday morning, I am once again with the grief of Anatole's loss, his loss, the loss of his feet, his walk. There were tears on Paula's face as I told her about Anatole's walk.

My obsession now is with expensive underwear and having silk next to my skin. I want to treasure and take care of my body. This week I have learned from Jeff Sullender, a nutritionist and holistic health practitioner, that I am weak and vulnerable. I must do more to take care of myself in order to develop real health and strength. Not just rely on momentum and the ability to push and do, which is like relying on the mechanics, on the automatic capacity to function—like driving a car without changing the oil.

. . .

A sugar packet, two alcohol preps in their foil envelopes, one yellow surgical glove, various magazines, a few catalogues. Then in a separate bag, a J. Crew sports shirt, unopened cologne. Presents sent to my dying husband by my sister. Never used but their message of hope, of recovery still clinging to them. A bill from a plumber. These things all in a wrinkled brown shopping bag that has been in the back of my husband's closet for these two years, five months, and twenty-one days. Today, finally, I am able to sort these items. I am keeping the issue of the *New York Times Magazine* that had his doctor-patient article.

When he was waking up from the anesthesia following the surgery, Anatole made a remark about being in the pocket of the Japanese emperor. The nurses thought his mind was off, but it was his irony surfacing. How like Anatole to be thinking about how the *Times* had tucked this seminal piece of writing into the folds of an inane, to his way of thinking, article about an overweight Japanese potentate whose girth had graced the cover.

There was also the Smith & Hawken catalogue. Some days before his operation Anatole and I had pored over its pages discussing the clothes and found this oddly comforting. Why this coming back to the last days of his life, why now?

At the clinic in Stoneham with a half-hour wait between clients, I have a choice of writing for myself or writing to a friend. I choose myself. These past days have been difficult. They have been a reprise of Anatole's dying. His "goneness" clangs through my days. I am missing how he moved, how he danced, how he lounged. Over the weekend I was down in New York working with Carol Southern, doing the final editing on the *Kafka* manuscript, Anatole's unfinished memoir of his life in Greenwich Village in the fifties. I slept on the living room couch overlooking Central Park on the eighth floor. Quietly, before Carol awoke, I would make oatmeal and tea in her kitchen and sit by the window and watch a flaming sunrise over city and park. Last time here, three weeks ago, working on this book, I was crazed with fear, not knowing how it would come together. Carol thinks it is. I don't know.

Driving back to Cambridge on Sunday, I stopped in Connecticut and saw Malcolm and Fran. A do-si-do, a reversal of roles. This time it is Fran with the cancer that has invaded her bones. Anatole's cancer went initially to his ribs. Fran's to her sternum. She talks straight. She speaks of the despair that comes and goes. She doesn't know what triggers it. No one knows what triggers cancer. It just happens and intrudes in the coursing path of our lives.

Malcolm comments, "Well, you haven't gotten to the gain that follows despair." Fran says coldly and clearly, "There is no gain." Fran is smart. She's brave enough to remain smart. Coming home later that afternoon, I begin to search through Anatole's closet for the small tape recorder we had in the hospital. I remember Vera, my friend, saying that a woman she knew had taped the voice of her dying husband but that she waited two years before she dared to listen to the recording. I thought at the time, Well, I won't wait. But I have. And even now I'm not sure I'm ready to hear Anatole's diminished voice.

Instead I found the photographs that Andrew Arkin, a life-long friend, took ten days before Anatole died. There is a picture of myself and Bliss hovering near Anatole's head, my arm on the pillow around his black hair, my eyes fastened on his eyes, which are looking blankly forward, their focus forced by the drip drip of the morphine into his bloodstream, his nerves, his soul.

Why do I still believe he died of starvation and not cancer?

Open Circle

On a gray March day I find myself on a smallish plane, five seats across, flying from Minneapolis to Rochester. Crutches are stowed in the overheads on this journey to Lourdes. Travelers from former pilgrimages recognize and greet one another. "We left home at seven-thirty," says the couple from Lexington, Kentucky. "We didn't leave till ten," respond the sisters from Pittsburgh. Grimaces, bursts of laughter, broad Midwestern "a" sounds. These noncoastal Americans return home to the shrine of medicine they trust, the Mayo Clinic.

My flight from Boston to Minneapolis was a half hour late. Motorized carts met passengers with connecting flights. I was asked if I could walk when my destination became known. As I am well, I hiked the long concourse with carry-on bags over my shoulder. I am going to Rochester to be on a panel about illness and dying. Excerpts from my husband's book, *Intoxicated by My*

Illness, will be read by Jason Robards. Once again I will think about Anatole and his doctors and his struggle with cancer, and my heart will ache, and I will try to say something on this panel that isn't shocking, something that is polite. I will be polite in gratitude for the fact that I did not grow up in the Midwest, that my speech, my gestures, my voice have been molded and modulated by the culture and reticence of New England and New York. I will be polite because I am not entrapped by sudden smiles, jerks of the head, amber plastic and gold-toned eyeglass frames, and red lipstick.

Why am I so snooty with this conviction that I'm better, smarter, more worldly, more sophisticated because I grew up in the East? Even though my early summers were all in Minnesota, I escaped. I have traveled. I married an exotic man. Anatole was a challenge and being with him inspired me to redefine myself and find an animation that is my own. I am proud and not always humble and even a bit nasty at times.

This is my second visit to the Mayo Clinic. As a small child I came with my mother and father to visit my dying grandfather. Leaving Rochester that day, I remember I lay down on the back seat of the car and looked upward out the side window to see only telephone poles, telephone wires, and occasional trees. Now I sit up in a narrow seat and look out over a cirrus sea of sunlit clouds, which remind me of the cotton wool of Virginia Woolf's line, "underneath or between or all around is that art of lives lived." We begin the slow dive down through these clouds to the art of my husband's words and Mr. Robards's voice. The sky has shadings of pale pink and blue, the beginning of a sunset. The plane has landed exactly on time. I realize that this is part of the art and so are my companions on the plane. Their exuberant voices, full-throated and friendly, embrace and clasp their lives to their hearts. They are reaching out and holding hands together, for they all have need of support.

I am met by a driver and taken to the Kahler Plaza Hotel. The chambermaid, who is from Mauritius, tells me that she worked in the penthouse suite when the Shah of Iran was a guest. There are swimming pools on miscellaneous floors. One sees children and adults barefoot and dripping in the elevators and hallways.

Mary Adams Martin has invited the participants for dinner. She lives far enough away that we go by car. There is snow on the ground, and the night air is frigid. I am prepared with my down coat and boots. No one else is bundled up. From a heated portico we are taken in an already warmed car to a driveway and walk that are dry and clear. In downtown Rochester everything is connected by skyways. People go from their heated garages to heated carparks. Coats aren't needed.

The dinner is a buffet. The food is excellent and the doctors and organizers of this event are friendly and outgoing. Jason Robards and I form a bond in that Anatole and I had lived in the same Connecticut village where he and his wife reside. I used to walk our dogs past his house. Our children attended the same school.

A couple introduce themselves to me. She's a psychologist and he a retired surgeon. They had read some of my writing that accompanied the background material I had sent ahead to Mayo. They compliment me on what I wrote and give me examples of what they had particularly enjoyed. I flush with pride, hearing this response from people whom I've just met. We agree to have lunch the following day.

Martin Adson is a second-generation Mayo doctor. His specialty was oncology. Now he's working on developing a program for medical students that will enhance their humanitarian skills in caring for patients. His wife, Pat, helps him with this program. She also has a private psychotherapy practice. Martin says over lunch that he believes that his skills as a surgeon were strengthened by getting to know his patients, who they were and how they lived. So simply said. That's all Anatole wanted. That's why he wrote his piece. I want to reach across the table and embrace this man. Lay my head on his shoulder and say, Why couldn't you have been Anatole's doctor? Instead I simply say, "I envy your patients."

For two nights the large auditorium is filled to hear Robards's monologue of Anatole's words. The reading has been staged by Isaiah Sheffer of Symphony Space in New York. There is a kinship between Anatole and Jason Robards. Jason says that he lived in Greenwich Village in the fifties and probably hung out in some of the same places as Anatole. They knew the same scene. In their respective crafts, they both confront mortality.

The reading is followed each night by a panel discussion. To speak in front of such a large group is not easy for me, but I manage and at one point actually say something that gets a small laugh. Something about Anatole being criticized for giving a book a harsh review, but then I say, "The author should have written a better book."

Leaving Minnesota, I realize that part of who I am is these people that I've been with for the past four days. Their friendliness, their availability is appealing.

One more weekend in New York with Carol Southern to complete the final edits on the *Kafka* book gets me out of my Cambridge house by seven on a cold Saturday morning. As I drive west out of Boston there is snow blowing off the car, frozen plates of ice scudding away, softened by the sun, creaking before they break off, like the encasements of grief.

This issue continues, this issue of I, we, our, my. Whether to say this "is" or "was" Anatole. I sense that "is" is right. He remains, his spirit, his presence, not his body, or his voice, or his smell or sounds, but Anatole continues to be felt, noticed. Adjustments are made to suit his idiosyncrasies.

Sitting in a coffee shop at Madison and Ninety-eighth I want to cry. My feet are heavy. I have a long day in front of me. This new me, the vivacity, the liveliness, the ever-engaging outward energy is tiring. I want to be alone in Sandy Lodge, walking the dogs and not hearing about how few copies of *Intoxicated* are selling. The effort required of all these things I'm doing is huge. It feeds me, but it also exhausts me.

The work with Carol goes well. The book has emerged. The story of Anatole in Greenwich Village right after the war—finding a place to live, finding himself, enmeshed in the vigor and headiness of modern art and modern literature—has found its shape.

The classes in the barn continue. The theme today, an open circle. With my hands I push down on my body while slowly standing up. Being upright leads to throwaway movements, small unconnected flicking gestures with hands and feet, sudden shifts of direction and level, as if to say, "So? So, what's next?" A quizzical acceptance. "Well, we'll see. I'll see with time. It's not so important. I'm not so important. I'll just do what I can do. It's okay. I'm okay."

Isolation. Ice. So . . . elation. Moving, being seen, being in a group brings an end to isolation. I recall the ice breaking off the car as I drove down to New York last week.

Saw a scene from *The Last of the Mohicans*. Todd had the video. Indians with no warning coming out of the woods and killing people on a train. This sudden violence, the killing, the death, is part of our heritage. Little boys play Cowboys and Indians. I have never been able to tolerate violence in movies, but I can be with this other kind of pain and slow violence.

I want to move on and away from all of these bad things and empty my life and my house so there is room for me. The stuff and belongings of my dead husband are bulging out, falling out of closets, drawers, boxes. Manuscripts, papers, socks, sweaters, shoes, books. I am crowded by all these things and yet I can't just dispose of them, toss them out, give them to Goodwill. I hang on to them as the remnants, the tangible evidence that, yes, I did have a husband. I once lived with a man. I shared a bed, a bathroom, a hallway, a chest of drawers, an attic with Anatole. If I empty all these places of him, what then? Is this the way to make room for myself?

If I clear all this out will I be able to expand and do more, be less overwhelmed, or will I be more distraught if I get rid of these belongings of Anatole's? It seems so wrong, and furthermore not possible, to toss away the jackets, the sweaters, the shirts that graced his shoulders, covered his back, wrapped his waist. I fear that with these things gone my images and memories of him will be less clear, and that would intensify my aloneness. If Brook were alive I could call him and rant and rave, not that he would have listened, but his voice would have helped, as would the familiar unpredictability of his responses.

Waiting in the lobby of a downtown Boston hotel for a seminar to begin—the topic is disengaged families—I'm sitting here looking at this gathering of social workers and always my eyes go the left hand, third finger. Is there a ring? I imagine the lives of the women I see. I remember mine as a wife, having a full-time job, a life with a husband, a home, a permanent home, a plan, vacations to look forward to, trips. Now it is all different. And this is why I sometimes feel that there is no necessity in my life. No "I do this because . . ." I could slide off my small place on this planet and never find a way to return.

Bliss read me her fan letter to Alice Munro. It was about her admiration for Munro's writing, but also about how she longs for, how she misses her father and how she continues to reach out and find him. One way is through Munro's stories. She writes that when something of Munro's particularly delights her she'll slap her thigh and know or hope that her father has heard.

At Paula's class this morning in the second improv my hands were groveling down my leg and then I slapped my thigh and remembered that this may be the only way that Anatole can hear his daughter. This morning's dancing has been about my children, their pain and their pleasures. I was delighting in how Todd talks to Michele, his new girlfriend, on the phone. "My body is out of control when I'm around you. It does these strange things. Did you notice I was shaking, short of breath?" How must she have felt when she heard these things. I am so proud of both my children.

Once again on standby.

An inexplicable traffic jam on Route 3 just before the Sagamore Bridge made many cars miss their reserved space and so the line is long at 6:20 p.m. I've been here two and a half hours. There are one hundred cars in line, unusual for a raw April Friday. I sit here and read my journal. I am not overly sad. I'm not crying. I'm worn, tired, and yet more confident of myself. Perhaps angry in a way, not so inspired. I'm flat but possibly more real. I am more carefree, willing to live whatever will be, although I fear I've become dulled. I have been sitting here reading a manuscript an acquaintance asked me to look at. Her subject is love. The basic premise is the distinction between love as an object and love as a verb.

The author's language doesn't breathe. It doesn't inspire, doesn't move me. I find this strange, as I'm on the edge or somewhere in between two relationships. Neither is serious, but both are curious. I don't want definitions or a guide map that advises, here do this, look for these signs, notice your language, is love a noun or a verb. It doesn't begin to describe or contain or even venture near what I had with Anatole. Many parts of our relationship were troubled. Yet a sense of mutual, triumphant love dominated. At the same time we both cherished each other and took each other for granted. We would simultaneously abuse and nurture our relationship. There was no clear formula or discernible path to our marriage. It was its own being, had its own shape, its own eccentricities, and was as cumbersome as it was delicate. We would toy and banter with our love and we would also stomp on it. Somehow we knew to trust its strength. We did not protect, nor did we husband our love. We took it for granted as a fact, a pact, a commitment between us. And we let ourselves rip with it. We acted out, we battled, we made up, we were coy, we were coarse.

At times we were bored by our love and yet it was always there waiting for us when we calmed down, when we returned to ourselves and to each other. I didn't know these things at the time. Only now do I see what I was living then.

And so I realize sitting once again in standby that our love, that assumption that supported our marriage, is still here, right here in this Plymouth Voyager, here with our two Labradors, our cat Belle, three animals breathing in their sleep, right here in this notebook, this pen with which I write these words, right here in the sweater I'm wearing, chosen from others in a store because I know it would have pleased Anatole. Because of this love Anatole is a part of me now.

How does this affect my life? What does this have to do with future loves or love in my life? Do I know what I'm doing? Do I need instruction in this matter of affections?

Another ferry arrives, its yawning mouth reaching, heading for its dock. Assured of its course it glides the last five feet to meet the wharf. The familiar berth, the familiar ropes and cleats, their knots once more hold the large boat while it changes passengers and cars.

I don't intend this boat to be a metaphor for the changing of partners in my life. Rather, as I sit here gazing at these ferries arriving and leaving, it is the assurance of doing the familiar thing that strikes me, and love is the familiar thing. So much of our day is about love, these small transactions that connect us to the world, to ourselves and to other people. So maybe what I'm writing about and feeling on this raw, cool final day of April two and a half years after Anatole's death is that this flatness, this lack of spark and vibrancy, is nothing but the surface, the flat bedrock of love. It's the place to return to, the place to rest, to stand by, to wait and to know that love has not disappeared. It is here supporting me, keeping me alive, keeping me going in the flat, dull places and on the rocky, high, slippery places where I fear hurt and feel pain. And as in my marriage, where the passion, the fire, the highs came and went, so will they now. I sit here, stopped, forced to stand still by the limited capacities of the ferries and remember back over the years and smile and chuckle and know that I've had my share of passionate kisses.

At ten-thirty my car rolls onto a freight boat. These flat-decked scows, built for no-frills transportation of trucks and cars, take up the slack when there is a long line of standbys. There's no snack bar and very limited indoor seating for foot passengers. Drivers stay in their cars.

There's no moon and the air has become chilled and damp with sea spray. There's a map-reading light just above the rearview mirror. I turn it on hoping that it won't drain the battery during the forty-five-minute voyage across Vineyard Sound. The dim light is just enough to see the scrawl my pencil makes. I consider the words that the pencil keeps forming.

I don't want to write a comforting book, or a consoling book. I want my words to be strong, to ring true, to reverberate with the pain and the hardness and the stink, the putrid stink of death. To be about the journey of a husband's death, the companionship on the way, the anger, the fracturing, the grotesque, the worst nightmares lived through, the defeat of it all, the end of it all, then the examination of what remains, what continues, and how that goes on. There is no cure, no answer, only the living of it, the telling of it. As Rich Ratzan, a doctor from Connecticut, says, all stories should be told. We talk from time to time about doctor-patient issues as he coordinates conferences that focus on the art of medicine. He often uses excerpts from Anatole's book *Intoxicated by My Illness*. Late at night he tells me about his frustration with time, with his teenage children as he's taking a break in the ICU in Framingham. I hear his story over the phone. I nod my head and say yes, children are like that. They exhaust. They make the parent unreasonably angry. It's hard to be a parent. It's tough to love and hard to die and we, as humans, need and want to hear again and again how the other guy does this, this business of living and dying.

When I was young, my mother would caution me, "It's not polite to talk about money." Better to keep quiet about something that might be upsetting. I grew up with knowing silences, aware of blank spaces that I could not fill with information that explained. As a child this made me want to explore. I searched the back of the drawers in my parents' bedroom, the highest shelf in the cabinet above the toilet in their bathroom. I thought I might find the stuff that was being withheld, being hidden. What I was not being told became treasure, so I hunted then and I hunt now, but now I search myself, my experience. I have this urge, I might even call it a passion, to say the ugly thing, the shocking thing. To slap down on the dining room table the douche bag I found high up above the toilet in my parents' bathroom, demanding an answer, an explanation. What's this? What do you do with this? Why were you hiding it? Screaming, Why can't you tell me? My parents died before they could tell me. Perhaps they planned never to tell me. Now, out of that early desperation, there is a need to tell everything. Still I am my parents' child, a loyal child, and I will not tell all. There is some of my experience, some of what I know that I will keep to myself. This keeping is a gift, a family tradition that I carry on, a gift to my children so that they can rail against me and their father and so be driven to dig and tell their stories, their truths.

Yesterday, while kneeling in the garden, dividing and transplanting perennials, I remembered the bench that our handyman, Frank, had made for us back in Connecticut. It was about five and a half feet long, constructed out of rough wood. Its solid, sturdy shape guaranteed it a long life out of doors. In Southport we had placed it under a pergola our son had made for two wisteria vines given to us by the local minister's wife. When we moved I remember envisioning it being placed under an oak tree on our Vineyard land. As I was kneeling, bending low over small plants, I realized that I had no idea where the bench was, that it had probably been lost in the move to Cambridge.

On the day that Anatole had his cystoscopy, which was the morning after the movers brought our belongings out of storage—we had to wait some weeks to get into the Cambridge house—that morning we looked around and realized that chairs were missing, a small table, andirons, and God knows what else. The movers were puzzled and seemed unable to figure out what had happened. I called our insurance agent. A week later more of our belongings were found and delivered, but responding to the shock of Anatole's diagnosis of cancer, we never checked through the numbered list of items and boxes of the mover's manifest. Only with time did I realize what was missing. A box with boat accessories, two of the four legs that unscrewed from a small table, a cane-and-steel chair that had been in my psychotherapy office, the garden bench, and who knows how many boxes of books. I never came across the silver candle snuffer that a friend had given us for our twenty-fifth wedding anniversary. What else had been packed with it?

I come to the Vineyard for many reasons, scenery, weather, and friends, but the most important reason is this experience of being alone. A day alone, talking only to the animals, being with myself. Who I am, what my experience is in life surfaces. It floats up like the memory of the lost bench. The image of this bench takes its place on the stage of my psychic dramas. As I go through the day the bench is joined by other losses. The Montblanc pen, perhaps twenty pairs of eyeglasses, earrings, my husband, my brother, houses no longer lived in. Disappearances. My life seen on this internal stage, unfolding when I am alone, is a story about disappearances. My parents, my boyfriend, my animals one by one, my trust in others, my competence.

Yesterday, by the end of the day I felt small, diminished, wrinkled, and folded into myself in response to remembering all these losses. I am a person who misses the mark, who forgets to send in for the refund, is late with bills, late with herself, misses the boat, ends up in standby. And then I am comforted by a message from my friend Joan. She calls my Cambridge answering machine and says she has neurasthenia so she's had to cancel all her obligatory social appointments. There is Joan, suffering unto herself, alone and nervous and yet she came in second for a Pulitzer Prize.

Woke at 3 a.m. Can't sleep. I want something or someone to take away this pain, a better word, more accurate word is *fault*, that I now live with. The plates of substance inside myself have slipped. There are dangerous empty places, chasms, crevices too wide to leap across. I don't know if I'm permanently damaged. I fantasize that a relationship with an interesting man would revive me or heal me. How I hate the word *heal*. I resist that word. Does this mean I resist, as they say, moving on? No, just keep the circle open.

Woods Hole parking lot, 6:45 a.m. Again in standby line, late June.

I've been here for a half hour. There are thirty cars ahead of me. Now, at a quarter to seven, more cars are piling up behind me. There are a lot of trucks, so I'll probably have a wait of a few hours.

I look at all these people beginning their vacations. Bikes and Windsurfing boards are tied to the tops of cars. Coolers, laundry baskets stuffed with clothes and towels are wedged in the way backs of vans and station wagons. I know they are living their dramas, these vacationing families, following the story line of their lives just as I am.

The woman at the parking lot booth greeting and sorting the

cars as they enter is so cheerful that I decide she must be on drugs.

Where am I? The men I've known as friends and otherwise are out of my life. Why do I begin by seeing myself in relation to a man? I am me. Solo. Alone. An individual operator with two dogs and a cat. I have my jobs, my responsibilities. I have my freedom, but what is that? It's many things. It is empty spaces, but also chores and possibilities.

Right now I'm sad and achy and tired, but this afternoon *Swallow*'s mast gets put in. I'm not a divorced woman, bitter and greedy. I'm thankful for that. I'm a widow, a young-looking widow who wants to live, to move, to dance, and to do social work. I want to build and write.

Alone, later in the day at Sandy Lodge, feeling tired and sad, thinking of Fran, the right side of her face fallen, deflated, already dead because of the pressure of the tumor in her brain. Remembering Anatole, his thinness, the swollen legs and feet. How a body distorts and deflates in these random ways. The internal rhythms, balance, and homeostasis disordered by cancer cause the body to unmold, literally lose the familiar shape, so that by which we recognize one's personhood becomes an image of horror. The misshapenness is the dying made visible.

I don't want to be with people. I want to be alone to feel this closeness with death—to be close to the bone of life, that which supports life, the dryness and the emptiness of the stillness of existence. As in the counsel of Ecclesiastes 7: "better to be in the house of mourning than the house of mirth."

The unavailable man was appealing because he was never around and he didn't ask questions, so I could keep these thoughts to myself. I know that I couldn't tolerate, I really couldn't stand the most wonderful man being in my life twenty-four hours a day. That would disturb and destroy this pond that I float in when I'm alone and where I sense feelings and words and bathe in my grief, surrender to the sadness I've known my whole life, allow it to seep through my pores, course through my veins. The indulgence of the enjoyment of its slime, the slippery worm feel of the shit of death, the rotting flesh, life no longer, the end of the day, eternal sleep, setting sun, the fiery glow spreading and fading in the low sky. Alone with the universe, I could easily slip and be sucked under by this mire. Instead I have been kept sane by the loud breathing, barks, and yips of two black dogs, who are always at my side and insist by tugging on their leashes on pulling me out into the world.

Standby

Got to Woods Hole at 9 a.m. Was told there would be a five- to six-hour wait. I don't care about being stranded. I find it comfortable to wait. I seem to be unable to move away from the grief. I have dug myself into the sandy cove of that place where I said goodbye to Anatole, to Brook, and now to Fran. The longing for these people, the desire for their voices, their flesh, their breath and touch keeps me sitting on this stretch of shore, this asphalt parking lot where my emptiness is not disturbed. Where it can, here, as I wait, settle through me. Where it is not pushed aside, told to be better, go away.

A ferry, the *Nantucket,* pulls out, the upper deck filled with holiday seekers leaning over the rails. A nine-year-old girl shouts to her father who is standing on the end of the pier, "Bye. See you later, alligator. Bye-ee!" But I can't say bye, see you later, as Fran did in her letter. After she died her husband, Malcolm, sent a letter to all her friends that she had written a few weeks before the end. She wrote about all the beautiful things in her life and said farewell, but tempered that by adding she'd wait for us on the other side. In the hard, dim places of my heart that word *goodbye* is followed not by the promise of a future rendezvous but by silence, a quiet that makes room for aloneness.

Here in the standby line I'm surrounded by families, groups of friends, packed into cars, bound for vacations. They have plans, an itinerary. I no longer make plans. If I do and then get a ferry reservation, I usually have to cancel it. I no longer know when it will be that I can move or travel. To have to follow a plan is torture of some sort now. I'm often tired. My fuel tanks are empty. I don't despair about this. I have a philosophical attitude about this indecisiveness. It's an opportunity to regroup or reshape myself, for that's what I need. The only thing that's clear for me is the dancing, the work with my body, the pleasure, the knowledge, the stroking and feeding that happens to the tissue, flesh, and bones as I work muscles and breathe, as I explore space, shape, and sense.

Today while sitting here I think about why I'm so stuck in my Cambridge house. Why I can't clean up the messes there, make phone calls, press for resolutions. But if I did that I would move forward. The debris has become my wailing wall.

Why is it that I want to kill anyone who wants to make me feel better? I want to scream and say, You insensitive, stupid person. You have no sense of what it is I feel, because if you did you wouldn't say those things. There is no help or distraction for me. You insult me. You insult the pain and loss if you think some pleasure will take it away. I have lost my coordinates, connections, the structure of my life.

In class yesterday Marcus spoke about not being melodramatic with the fierceness. He had given us a jagged, assertive phrase, center floor, and then commented that melodrama weakens the statement. I know that I do this. I know that these words are an indulgence. Later in class he warned that if you rush to connect with the passion of Igor's music you lose your timing. You feel rushed and you lose yourself. Slow down. Take your time. There is time to do what you need to do. Be careful with your edges. Be conscious of the words you choose. Yet I remember reading years ago the story of a woman, Mary Barnes, suffering with psychotic illness, who needed to smear her own shit, her own filth on walls before she got better. She went on to become a painter.

I want to write more, grab snatches of time to catch and preserve pieces of myself. I didn't write this summer about how bad I was feeling, missing Anatole, being alone, angry at friends. I got through July and August, however, and am less depressed, more settled, less torn. I hope for a friendship, a romance, an other to be with at least some of the time, but I know I need time alone to work, to write, to sort, to arrange my world.

Driving to Andover today I realized that there was no one in my life who wanted to know or would ask about how my day was. Not that Anatole was very interested, but sometimes if I needed to, I would tell him and he would listen. At least there were ears in the house. Now I'm living the life of a hermit, but it's a hermit in disguise. It looks like, appears to be, that I'm surrounded by many people, but actually they're a cover for my solitude. My hermit existence is a secret that I keep to myself. Part of the reason that I'm angry with summer Vineyard friends is that they intrude on my hermit life. They are real and they can reach me, unlike my casual contacts in Cambridge. The strange and complicated thing is the answering-machine communications I have with other closet hermits, Joan and Jessica. We have this audio-machine intimacy that is born out of the need for our selves to be separate, to flutter alone in their own space, to bump up against the walls, doors, and windows of our habitats and of our histories. These dances and odd moves are done in private. We mine ourselves, like prospectors looking for gold.

. . .

Attended David Whyte's workshop today with Pat Adson, a seminar on soul, spirit, and poetry. Whyte is an inspirational speaker, a poet from Yorkshire who recites verse with the cadence and burr of a Presbyterian minister. I am skeptical about the merchandising of things of the spirit, yet his readings of Wordsworth and mention of the Lake Country brought me back to those moments on Haystacks halfway up when I first felt the dread of Anatole's illness.

The approach to the foot of the trail up Haystacks, a hike recommended by Wainwright in his guidebook, is a path between two fenced fields of lambs and ewes. As we walked between these pens of babies sucking at their mothers' bellies, one small black lamb became separated from his parent. Frightened and panicked, he dashed around, found an opening in the fence, squeezed through, and ranged farther away in search of the large familiar body that fed him. I tried to guide him back. The others, my husband and our friends, Suzy and Hugh, said, he'll be okay. There must be a shepherd who knows what to do. He'll reunite them. But I didn't see a shepherd.

As we began our assent I kept looking back, keeping an eye on what was now a small black speck coursing and searching along the outside edge of a pen. The lamb's panic became my panic. Just like this lamb, I had lost my mother while still an innocent. When she died I had been lost, shut out from family closeness. The anxiety of separation was familiar to me. It shackled my feet as they struggled to find footing on the rocky path. My steps were clumsy, and this unsteadiness made the lamb's fright more real for me. I knew I could not climb out of range of sight of the small nervous black speck.

Meanwhile my husband was complaining about the rocks in the path. He was sixty-eight and in excellent shape. An athlete, a runner, he rarely tired. He had looked forward to this hike, enchanted by Wainwright's description. "One can forget even a raging toothache on Haystacks." We had all speculated on what there would be in a landscape that could have such a healing, restorative effect. What would the nature of its composition be? Hidden crannies, views of mountain lakes, distant pastures?

After an hour of climbing a steep trail with loose rocks, we decided to pause and have lunch. That morning we had bought bread and ham, local cheese, and fruit at a village market. At that altitude, with the brisk spring air of early May, Anatole declared this to be absolutely the best food that he'd ever tasted. In fact this, he said, was the best meal of his life. I was still worried about the little lamb. The bread and cheese just seemed like bread and cheese to me. I noticed the incongruity of his declarations about the food and the complaints about the trail. He said he had no patience for the loose rocks, which made one's footing unsteady. He grumbled that walking up a beautiful mountain was a completely wasted experience if you had to keep looking down at your feet so as not to slip. He didn't want to go any farther. Hugh, sprightly as a mountain goat, was determined to get to the top. Suzy and I sensed a shadow near Anatole on this cloudless, brilliant day, and we also opted not to continue. Hugh went ahead and we stayed put and waited for his return. The lamb was continuing to distract me. I kept looking but could no longer see its whereabouts.

As I think back to that hillside, I sense the uneasiness I had with Anatole pulling back from a physical endeavor. On beaches he was always challenging those younger than himself to sprints. He would play paddleball for hours, never tiring. My memory is that he was tired, and that it was this fatigue and not the rocky footing that stopped him that day. Was he experiencing the first restraints of age? His mortality was palpable. He knew it, sensed it, and he knew that Suzy and I had seen. Perhaps the food for him was a kind of a last supper, the last lunch of his "no bars held" existence before the descent to his grave.

His doctor, a few weeks earlier, had already told him that there was a problem with his prostate, an elevated PSA, and advised him to check it out further with a urologist. I did not know this at the time. Anatole hadn't told me. We were to move in six weeks to another state, to Cambridge, Massachusetts. Overscheduled and overwhelmed with finishing up with our jobs and sorting and packing, we intended this trip to be a time to rest up, eat well, and refuel before the big transition. He waited until August to see another doctor. Had Anatole felt a clenching sensation below his bowels that day on Haystacks that told him that his time had run out, that his youth, his endless energy had left, that he was going to die? The doctor's information must have been a concern for him. His father had died of cancer.

None of these thoughts were conscious, of course, but they explain my preoccupation with separation that day. When we got back down to the fields of sheep, there was no bleating black lamb to be seen. He must have found his mother.

After the workshop Pat and I talk about the experience of listening to four hours of poetry, the thoughts and feelings that were evoked. Then, both knowing the wisdom of a balanced day, we drive into Boston for tea and a walk down Newbury Street, a reconnection to the pedestrian world.

As I go to sleep that night the poem that David Whyte had read about loss comes to mind. Gold coins at the bottom of a well. I drift to the memory of the fallen trees behind the Vineyard house. Trees uprooted, twisted branches, a woodland torn apart. The images sharpen the focus of my mind. Lying in bed I recall the darkened leaves on trees, leaves with no color, killed by whipping salt-laden winds carried inland by the August storm, Hurricane Bob, two years ago.

I wrote about the tangled wood, the destruction at the time, which was in the months following Brook's death. I remember driving in. The familiar view was like a war zone. Felled trees covered the two acres. The destruction of the trees was yet another loss, another part of my life destroyed. I wrote through the nighttime hours when I could not sleep, and then I lost the notebook in which I described the aftermath of my brother's death, the countless rides to Manchester, Vermont, the last few miles descending into the valley, his valley, his village, the weekly descent back into his life, to pick up the pieces he dropped as he fell, as he died almost instantaneously on a warm July afternoon while washing a car.

I've known about this lost notebook for two months but it has not bothered me until now. I recently told a friend who began law school two weeks after her mother died that she wouldn't lose or forget the experience of caring for her mother. She knows she needs time and solitude to swallow, absorb, digest the memories, the smells, the touch that lingers in her hands, her arms of the supporting, moving, and lifting and arranging as her mother grew weaker, as her mother's insides rotted and spilled and decayed. She wants to feel, think, cry, and write about what she did with her mother. I again say she won't forget. But have I forgotten?

Got to standby at 6:45 p.m. Seventy cars ahead of me on a late-September evening going back to the mainland. I wasn't sure I'd get off tonight. I ran toward the ferry terminal in a pelting rain to get a car ticket. By 7:45 a freight boat and the *Nantucket* had emptied the dock area. All that remained were sixteen cars and a U-Haul truck trailering a Jeep. The loudspeaker announced that we should return to our cars by 8:45 for the next freight boat. I went inside the terminal to read because I didn't want to wear down the battery in my car.

I realized that I'd forgotten my vitamins. It would be two weeks before I returned. To replace them would be $80 and I feel the difference when I don't take them. I called a neighbor, Howard, who offered to bring them down. As I was waiting for him I realized I couldn't find my ferry tickets. The envelope that I carry in my purse, which contains future reservations, was missing. My confidence crumbled. The normal starch of my viable self wilted and turned gray from overuse, failing eyesight, poor planning, scatter-brainosis, and "Sandy the sloth" daggers. I'm doing *too much!* Why all of this? The psychotherapy, the friends, the boat, the two houses, bills, maintenance, producing and editing books. At these moments I do not, clearly do not, as David Whyte suggests one should, I do not love that part of me that is ditzy, forgetful, messy, disorganized. I am appalled by my sloppiness. I yearn for order and predictability.

Yet today, at the meeting with twenty-nine people squeezed into my living room discussing a civic matter, there was great pleasure for me. These people are my neighbors, my community. I have a place, I have a life. I am a person here, as much a person without a mate as I was with Anatole. Is this my place, my context? Is it a withdrawal to be on the Vineyard more of the time?

As I write this, deep in my belly, as if at the bottom of a well, there are small heavings of grief that are disquieting, like the rolls of water that are pitching this freight boat upward and sideways. There's an occasional splash of salt spray rinsing the car. Liquid salted confetti thrown at the window as I clutch my pen and write in a notebook that is being held on the back of a frightened, trembling Lab who has wedged himself into my lap.

In class today, at the end, Marcus said to me that my line and form were there and the center floor work is becoming more confident when I stay with it. Marcus said this about those moves that at my age I'm not sure I should be attempting, like strenuous falls. The fact is I that I am doing them. He added that as I get tired I move better. This reminds me of the psychic who told me six years ago that I was a worker and advised me not to take vacations.

Once again in standby. Friday of Columbus Day weekend I confidently drive down into the Woods Hole parking lot expecting to get on the 2:45 p.m. boat only to discover that my reservation is for tomorrow. There are one hundred fifty cars ahead of me and a predicted wait of five hours.

I park the car illegally in front of the fast-food stand. The parking lot is jammed with families, dogs, cars, suitcases, backpacks. I go in to the ticket counter and try to plead a mistake, but then I clearly see my handwriting on the ticket, which I had changed six weeks ago. Saturday, 2:45 p.m.

I was to have met my builder and an architect at my house at 4 p.m. I have been looking forward to this meeting all week— the beginning of my plan to build a winterized addition onto the uninsulated Vineyard house. This will be my eventual home. My future. But I won't be there. I frantically begin to make credit-card calls to the Vineyard, each time pressing twenty-eight digits. I often miss and have to start again, trying to find a neighbor who can leave a message at my home for the builder. I keep pressing the wrong numbers, blinking back tears of disappointment, and have to restart the dialing process again and again as my mistakes multiply. Finally I locate a neighbor who will leave a message.

I go back to the car and settle down for the wait. I realize I've lost my glasses. They are nowhere in the car. I go back to the ticket office and they're not at the counter or at the phone. I can't ask about them because now tears are flooding the corners of my eyes and if I talk I will end up sobbing.

This weekend is the third anniversary of Anatole's death. The weather has changed back to summer warmth, reminding me of the final long days of Anatole's life and the morning drive alone to the hospital, crying in the closed-windowed car.

Abandon hope all ye who enter here, Marcus commented at the beginning of class yesterday. I remember how I had to have hope. Hope that Anatole would survive, beat the cancer, not die. I couldn't allow, couldn't admit that Anatole might die. I couldn't be with him in those times and places where he had no hope.

Hope continues for me. This addition, which will make it possible for me to have heat and water in the winter, is hope. I believe it can happen even though I don't have the funds to build it. The architect was returning to Boston, so we meet in the parking lot here. His ideas for the new portion of the house do not fit with my vision. I decide that when the time comes, I will work directly with my builder, trusting my own sense of proportion and space.

Rowing

I saiah Sheffer and Jason Robards are collaborating again. This time at Symphony Space in New York. Isaiah extrapolated a monologue from *Kafka Was the Rage* and has combined that with the *Intoxicated* reading that Jason did at the Mayo Clinic. The light and the shadow of Anatole's life, his youth and his demise. It is a grand pairing, Anatole and Mr. Robards. The opening night will double as the book party for *Kafka*.

My friend Kai, who lives outside of Cambridge, comes down to New York with me. She's a keen, no-nonsense observer who will be a good reality check after this is over. Somehow there ends up being very little publicity about this event in the New York press. I am feeling paranoid since the *New York Times* gave *Kafka* such a negative review that Rebecca Sinkler, the editor of the Sunday *Book Review*, called in advance to warn me.

Bobbie Crosby, my high school friend, lives in New York as

well as the Berkshires and invites me to stay at her house on the East Side. We are more like sisters than friends, as Bobbie and her family literally took me in after my parents died.

After the reading I am numb, unsettled, pleased yet oddly empty and sad. No feeling of victory or triumph. At the reception following the performance a woman says to me, "You're a lucky person." What? Lucky to have had a talented husband? Lucky to be hearing a famous actor read his words? I didn't get it. I want to say something, but I can't. I only stammer, Yes.

This evening is not my life. My life is my work, seeing clients, dance classes, cleaning the kitchen sink, sailing in *Swallow,* mowing lawns, hugging the dogs, cleaning up the perennial messes, moving things from place to place, doing the laundry. Take me away from that for half a day and I long to be back there, back to the familiar territory that is the busyness, the texture, the annoyance of the everyday, my well-worn paths of habitual routines. The evening was moving, but I prefer Anatole's words in a more intimate way, on a page, in a book held in my hands, in my lap, close to my face, to my eyes. The quietness and solitude of that, as in Stevens's poem.

> *The house was quiet and the world was calm.*
> *The reader became the book.*

This public reading is an embarrassment for me. It takes something I have known in private and makes it public. I resent its use as entertainment. Now that he's gone, what remains, his words and memories, are somehow sacred to me. I want what's left to be only with me, to reside deep, deep inside me, because there are some things that as his wife of thirty years only I know.

Then this other, this publicized Anatole can go on wherever he happens to go, but I will not follow. I am not so interested in the public Anatole. What moves me, what concerns me, what interests me is the part of my husband that stays with me and becomes me. That part will change me and allow me to go on and continue my life.

Some weeks ago I'd browsed Anthony Storr's book *Solitude*. He is a British psychoanalyst who writes about the virtues and rewards of being alone, of which there are many. I agree, and I would also add my "hermit theory" of how we who isolate, who choose to live and work alone, how we in our empty rooms roam about. The energy of our emotional selves propels us as we push and search for new horizons.

Leafing through Evelyn Waugh's *The Learning Years,* I come across Anatole's check marks in the margins. These small pauses while he was reading, seeing them is like a brief one-way conversation with Anatole.

his annoyance at being cautioned or warned

All my life I've sought dark and musty seclusions like an animal preparing to whelp.

yearning for an earlier age

Driving back to Cambridge from New York, I stop in Mamaroneck to see Bobbie's mother, Janis. She is going through a particularly bad spell of failing health. We are in her kitchen, Janis slumped in a low lawn chair, taking up most of the space in the small, cluttered, but carefully ordered room, myself on a step stool wedged next to the stove, hovering near Janis's right ear. Much of the time her eyes are closed. I just sit and wait. I fix myself a simple dinner and warm up some leftover lasagna for my ailing friend. That's what she wants, but she can't eat at nine o'clock.

Only later at eleven does she attempt to feed herself and she slowly finishes the small portion. She regains some strength. I pick up a J. Crew catalogue and begin to browse through it. Janis says it always looks good in the catalogue, but it's not so good when it arrives. I continue to turn the pages and then Janis asks me if I'm lonely. I say, yes, sometimes. I ask her if she has been. Her husband, Albert, died eighteen years ago. She says, "Oh, at times, but mostly I've kept myself very busy."

She asks me to hand her one of her bedtime medications. There is also a small orange vial of Elavil, an antidepressant. I ask her if she wants one of these. She says no. Then goes on to talk about an article she read in the *Wall Street Journal,* which said that the most common cause of suicide among the elderly was a combination of depression and pain. I ask Janis if she wants to die, if she would kill herself. She says no, but that she knows how she would do it. She would take a lot of pills and then sit in her car with the motor on in her garage. We talk more about pain. Then Janis says she never thought it would be like this. I take that to mean the weakness, shortness of breath, the dull constant pain, the inability to putter, to be entertaining, to be pretty. I remembered Janis used to get massages. I wondered out loud if that would help. She said no. I responded that I was thinking of a very light, soft massage. She said, "I don't like to be touched." I said, "Really . . . except by your dogs." She laughed and agreed. "I don't like to be touched. I never have and I don't know why."

On the refrigerator in the Vineyard in small newspaper print there's a quote from Grace Slick. "I'm not interested in having people touch me unless they want to have sex with me. I like the Japanese method of bowing. I'm Norwegian. What do you expect."

Some weeks later I'm sitting at my Cambridge desk, adding up figures, trying to get a sense of my tax position. Punching in the numbers on my calculator and getting totals of income and expenses, I come face-to-face with what there is and what there is not to support myself and these two houses. Again I realize that I go from day to day with the assumption that I'm upper-middle-class and so I will be supported and that I can shop in good stores, wear only fine shoes. My elegance doesn't waver.

But now, having to sit still, add these figures, look at the black-and-white of these columns of numbers, I know that I must begin to make some hard decisions about this house.

Another new year has begun. My sister hears the worry in my voice and says she'll pay for an airline ticket to Florida. A change of scene, some distractions, she says, will help. The travel agent I call finds a low fare, so I just put it on my charge card.

After passengers board the plane at Logan and go nowhere, the captain says, "Sorry for the delay, but here in the cockpit there were generated various spurious indications that we needed to adjust."

To pass the time I pull out my notebook. As I retrieve a pen from my purse I realize that the sunglasses that I'd carefully put in the Florentine glasses case that Bliss had bought for me are gone. They were in the pocket with the three letters I had mailed earlier at the airport. They could have fallen out there or perhaps they fell out in the car when I pulled out my wallet to get a dollar for a T token when Todd dropped me off at Harvard Square. These were the glasses that Anatole had picked out for me. Round red frames. I don't know how I could have been more careful. Each small loss has its jet-stream trail of former losses. Significant and insignificant, they all tear a part of me away.

I know this about me and about living that these things, these objects, these people pass in and out of my life very fluidly. I am not startled by their disappearance, but still I am saddened. Red-framed sunglasses, the look, the feel of them in the hand, on my face, they were a reference point to memories, details that fill out, flesh out a personal history.

Yesterday Kai said in response to my writings—she'd just reread some of my pieces—that they made her sad. Sad to read about so much pain. Is that what I want in this book? My training and work as a therapist is to help patients stay with their pain. I wonder if I am limiting my focus to the dark side only, the cloistered, dimly lit soul anguish that I know and that in turn my patients know, or I help them to know when they come to me. As my role as a therapist is to listen and be present, to substantiate, validate their pain, so for me this writing, these words are sentinels to my inner caves of the heart. That phrase not mine but rather a title of a work by Martha Graham, *Cave of the Heart,* in which Medea confronts her own darkness. The other Graham work that explores this dangerous territory is *Errand into the Maze.*

There is a long serpentine rope. On one end a minotaur, the other, a woman coiling back on herself, retreating along the path of the rope. When Bliss was five years old I took her to a studio performance of *Errand,* and as we began the drive home to Connecticut from East Sixty-third Street, as we got onto the East Side Highway, I asked her what she thought the stories were of the dancing we'd seen. In her squeaky voice she told me that the woman was dancing her fear. I was stunned by her reply, that her young eyes could see so clearly.

This morning, as I arrived at Gate 3 of the Northwest terminal at Logan airport in the midst of snow that had been falling through the night, a plane was being deiced. Two trucks with cherry pickers were backed up to the plane and the operators in red wool caps and blue work suits were aiming a hose device at the tail fin and wings of the plane. Slow-motion smoke rose from the antifreeze solution that was being sprayed over the fuselage, leaving the metal shiny and slick. Nearby there were trucks and tractors of all sizes and shapes, cars, vans, snowplows large and small, men in navy and red waving, signaling to one another, in the distance a plane taxiing to the one runway that was open. It was Richard Scarry's *Busy, Busy World* come to life. These were the children's books that most delighted Anatole, Todd, and Bliss. So much activity on each page. "What's this? What's he doing? What's she doing?" our kids would ask, their eyes scanning the busy pages crowded with people and vehicles and buildings. Anatole liked these books because they reminded him of city street life. So much to see, to do, to notice. So many questions to ask.

I looked out the airport windows for a long time, pleased and amused by all this human activity and also reassured by it, the teamwork, the purposefulness of it all, the necessary nature of each of those jobs. The mundane poetry of this moving mosaic creates a stability, a predictability that balances the randomness of loss.

I too am employed and so I am also a chip in this mosaic. Making appointments, showing up for work that I really like. It connects me to the world of my community, and this is my salvation.

These Richard Scarry books portray civilization in its most homey and immediate form, not as fine art, great symphonies, or majestic buildings but as the minutiae of daily activity. And these minutiae, the specific details of daily work, are the blood flow that supports life, supports achievement. They are the underpinnings of all grand enterprise and as such have the most poignant of all value because they contain the most intimate and most unacknowledged kind of beauty, which perhaps only fathers and small children cuddled together see, the colorful page lit by the low light of a bedside lamp.

No longer fretting over the lost sunglasses, I recall the moment yesterday of triumph and joy. My accountant called. He was pursuing two requests from the Commonwealth of Massachusetts for back taxes. He asked me to find two canceled checks, one from 1990 and one from 1991. In the past this would have sent me into a tailspin.

I have one hour free today to tie up loose ends before this trip. I can't search for them. I'll never find them. I'll just have to pay the $3,000. Instead I found them in three minutes. I wouldn't have been surprised to hear Beethoven's Fifth on NPR. The small daily shuffling, filing, and sorting, those tedious tasks that feel like irritations, are beginning to work. I can't believe it's happening. I like it.

Once again waiting in a doctor's office, this time for my son, Todd, twenty-nine years old, worried about cancer because of an enlarged node under his right arm. My paranoia, his paranoia, a low-burning fire because of all the cancer in both my family and Anatole's. My father, my grandfather, myself, Anatole, his father, and his sister. My aunt Lillian died of leukemia at twenty-five. Although today I know, I believe that a systemic treatment of cancer can reverse it, so my fear no longer has the panic of when Anatole was diagnosed, because I truly believe that Todd has the capacity to do what my friend Barbara Jensen has done. My fear is for the interruption of Todd's life and mine. But as I write that last sentence I realize that if the worst is true, then this is my life, this is Todd's life. These very hard things are the terrain, the shape of what our lives are. I live in Cambridge, this city of Victorian houses with flaking paint, its urban mix of peoples, the poor, the brainy, a city where you put your shoulder to the wheel.

The test results a few days later report a viral infection, not cancer.

Friday night in Cambridge, I'm working at my desk, finally getting some insurance paperwork organized. At 7:15 I go downstairs to fix some dinner. I turn on the radio, more to hear the weather report than anything else. Snow began again this afternoon but is now a wet drizzle. There is what I call club music on WGBH. Dancey blues, stompy music. The kind that gets you out of your seat and onto the floor at a nightspot. A hand and a smile from your partner and then you move into the music. I've always loved that moment, the beginning of what you know will be a good dance set. Now with this earthy music I'm dropped down suddenly, completely into my sadness. It closes over my head as I begin to make a simple meal for myself.

The sadness tells me I'm alone. I have no one to dance with. No more rock and roll on a Saturday night. The sadness forms pools by my unmoving feet as I tear lettuce for a salad. No more early movies on a Sunday night. No more dinners with another couple on Friday nights. Yes, there will be lunches, brunches with friends, mostly women friends, but evenings, as the sadness swells around my feet, will be mine, alone, either working or putting together a simple meal to take up to my bed, to place on a bed tray so as I eat I can watch an unfamiliar TV show halfway through. The TV actors' voices and images there just so I'm not completely alone. I don't even listen to the plot line. Mainly I notice their hairstyles, the clothes they wear, how their voices sound. The sadness swirls up around my legs, arms, torso. My heart, now like a sponge, soaks up the wet. Melancholy pulls the cloudy moisture into itself, sodden like the March landscape outside the kitchen windows, with its winter-long snow, gray with city grime, melting into the cold ground, forming dark, muddy ruts around foot and paw prints. Too much water for the earth and too much sad wetness for my heart. Without Anatole, without my husband, the sadness tells me, reminds me, that I'm alone, cast off, on a solo voyage now. Every night, every end of day is a solitary time. Every morning, every awakening is only to my own thoughts, my own questions, my own lack of answers.

My ancestors were Norwegians. The land of the midnight sun is also the place of the endless night, so I don't fear this cold, wet darkness. My Viking forebears had the courage, the curiosity, the tenacity, the lack of foresight to set off in their long, narrow boats, sail past Greenland to the unknown, unimagined, unconceived in the twelfth century, two hundred years before Columbus.

On this chilled damp night, ice once again is setting up by the back steps and in the ruts made by tires in the driveway. With the damp cold air seeping in past the poorly sealed edges of the north-facing windows over my desk, I have a body sense, a body memory of my forebears huddled in their open boats on the

North Atlantic, set on their course, rowing when there was no wind. It was not a question of courage or bravery, this voyaging into uncharted seas where there was neither knowledge nor guarantee of landfall. It was simply what they did. They were Vikings. They pushed forward. They explored. They traveled far from home. When the sadness is especially cold and damp, then I remember this Viking part of me and know that this is something I can do, the lonely rowing into the dark night of myself.

My mother was born in Kensington, Minnesota, and lived there the first seven years of her life. A family story, a true story, is that for many years, those first years of my mother's life, my grandfather had as a footrest under his desk a large stone, the Kensington Runestone. In 1897 a nearby farmer, while clearing a field, found under the roots of a tree a large rectangular stone with runic characters chiseled into one side. My grandfather together with a group of five other businessmen in town purchased the stone and became its caretakers, and it resided under my grandfather's large rolltop desk. Over the years it was examined by linguists and experts who studied and analyzed the writings. There was much controversy about its authenticity. The years when it was believed to be a hoax the stone served as a footrest for my six-foot-tall grandfather. Under his tie-up high leather shoes the runic characters told this story.

"Eight Goths and twenty-two Norwegians on exploration journey from Vinland throughout the west, we had camp beside two skerries one day's journey north of this stone. We were out fishing one day, after we came home, found ten men red with blood and dead. Ave Maria. Deliver from evil. Have ten men by the sea to look after our ship fourteen days journey from this island. Year 1362."

They left their words. Far from their family hearths these men needed to tell their story.

Moving

The end of winter hangs on. Gray days. The temperature hovers in the high thirties. Wet winds make it feel colder. Various people have told me about a psychic in Lexington. Margot Schultz. She teaches classes in channeling and tuning in to your psychic powers. I call and make an appointment. I want to push around the next corner, but need a nudge, perhaps some guidance. I want to be able to recognize the next corner. She schedules me for eight on a Monday morning. I wake up with a terrible cold, but have no thoughts about canceling the appointment. I prepare by writing down questions. What direction should my work go in? Should I sell my house? Where am I in this emotion of grief? Will it begin to ease off now? I don't want to ask her about the possibility of a man in my life. Somehow that is too personal a question for a woman who is a stranger to me.

I find the house easily and am ushered into a small sunroom

and sit across a square table from her. My list is in front of me. Margot begins talking immediately after she pushes the start button on her tape recorder. She had told me to bring a blank tape along. There's a long prologue about the universe, stars to guide, being in harmony. I tune out and then she says that my husband wants to apologize for being so selfish in this life and always focusing on his own needs. He did this, she says, because he had finally found his voice. Then she goes on to tell me how in past lives he had protected me. In Spain, in the Dark Ages, we were both monks at a monastery. An edict had been issued to destroy all the books, and it became our work to transfer the knowledge of these books to an oral tradition, to memorize them and find others to do the same. I tended to be outspoken about the repressive laws then in effect, and numerous times Anatole had saved my hide by covering up for me and intervening with the authorities. So I suppose I owed him in this lifetime. I did appreciate the apology, however.

The psychic tells me that my work now will be more with groups. She sees me working in the Southwest somewhere. As I hear this, I think, Well, that's off the mark, because I would never move away from the East Coast because of the Vineyard and I am forever reluctant to leave the animals to sitters. By this time she had gleaned that I am a social worker. My skepticism about psychic intuition is now overshadowing the aptness of Anatole's apology, yet I continue to listen, the tape turning slowly in the small cassette. There is more about the universe, intention, growth, and change. Then Margot begins to talk about my house. She tells me that I need to get it in shape to sell, because even though I might not move for three years, there could be at a moment's notice an opportunity for a better house, one more appropriate to my needs, and I would have to move swiftly to make this happen. This is Margot's real bull's-eye, although I don't know it at the time. She never really talked about the sadness and when it would lighten. Although I realized later that Anatole's apology had been timely, so like him to do it after the fact, and funny in a way, so that I felt that, okay, I did what I needed to do with him and now I can go on and pay attention to my own life.

The strange thing is that a few weeks later my real estate agent, who's also a friend, calls and says that if I want to sell, there is a brief window in the market for a house like mine since there is nothing in my price range, and in her opinion I have a good chance of selling at the asking price. I had heeded Margot's advice and straightened out the closets, the basement, had some funky ceilings repainted and pared down miscellaneous objects in rooms for a cleaner, more orderly presentation. In the previous six months my agent friend had shown me some two-family houses, and I knew that this was what I needed, to own a home that would give me some income and flexibility. In two weeks Wendell Street is sold above the asking price and I have bought a three-family house on Frost Street a few blocks away. My plan is to gut the upper two floors and make a three-bedroom home for myself with an office for clients and rent out the first floor. If I ever need more income I can move downstairs and rent the larger space, and so be able to cut back on my workload. Financial clouds are beginning to clear.

With this new house I'm moving away, really moving away from Anatole, my marriage, my past life, my self who was a wife to Anatole, my self who was a supporter of others. Now my primary job is to support me. So it is not only familiar walls I'm leaving, it is a lifestyle, a way of being that six months from now will be in the past. I feel my self changing, shivering, raw nerves sounding these spring days like a somber obbligato, which is saying goodbye to old ways and old contexts.

This is a good move for me. I am basically happy about it and yet there is this heaviness and resistance. Hicks comes to mind, our large white Lab, who wedged himself between the garbage cans as we were moving from one house to another in Connecticut. Not wanting to change houses, not wanting to learn a new environment, this placid dog snapped at me, the only time ever in his life, when I urged him into the car for the final trip to the new home. I too feel wedged between my garbage. I want to leave it behind but am not sure I can part with it.

Coming to Woods Hole with no reservation, I'm aware that before crossing Vineyard Sound there will be time and stillness where I can sink within myself. I park the car in the line of standbys. In the ferry terminal I pick up a newsletter for tourists, filled with ads for boat charters and real estate. I go get coffee and a doughnut. On paper I begin to try to place furniture in the new house. The move is in three weeks. I know my writing notebook is in the car and yet I'm not reaching for it. As I walk back from the food store, tears push through my eyes.

The 9:45 boat pulls out filled with happy passengers. People related in twos and threes. I keep assuming that there are no lonely people on these ferries. I know that can't be true, but it's what I see. Perhaps those of us who are sad in this brilliant blue morning air fade beside the bustle of our fellow travelers. There are too many bicycles, so I can't get on. Another hour to wait with eyes damp for past summers, past contexts. Again and again this happens to me in this parking lot. Yet I fiercely protect my independence, my whims of arrival and departure.

Walking back from the food store, I once more, perhaps for the sixth time, thought of the final scene of last night's dream. I woke this morning at six, too uncomfortable and frightened to stay in the dream. As I walked down the main street of Woods Hole, it occurred to me that perhaps this is how I died in a previous life.

I was walking, traveling a great distance out onto Long Island in the seventeenth century before anything had been built there. I knew that on the south side of the island there were great beaches. No one else seemed to know this. The land I walked through was flat and barren. It felt good to be so close to these wonderful beaches, beaches that were still empty. There was water between me and the beaches, like the water of Chilmark

Pond. I saw a pineapple shell, a large one, half of it, floating in the shallow water, a small prickly boat. I waded out and picked it up and hurled it toward the beach, realizing that people hadn't yet thought to ferry themselves across the bay to what lay beyond. The sky was overcast, gray and murky, no sun, no shadows. I looked around, back to where I'd come from. There was water in every direction. I was standing thigh-deep in the water. The tide was rising. There was no way to tell my direction. I knew I could drown. I stood still and tried to figure out a way back to safety, to figure out a way by looking at the tide, the wind direction, the current, but I had no charts, not enough knowledge, too few coordinates.

Perhaps this is why I want to become confident on the water, to know how to survive on the water. But in a more pragmatic way this dream tells me of my current life. That I am wandering, dreaming of beaches while the tide is rising—the tide in my life being how I hold on to debris and tolerate disorder. I walk away, turning my back on New York, the city, business, the predictable grid of streets to daydream.

Clarence A. Barnes III and his guys, movers from the Vineyard, arrive to lift, carry, and organize furniture and boxes so that it can be stored in the basement of the new house on Frost Street, as the renovation of the top floors begins immediately. Clarence— or Trip, as he's known on the island—is a one-man circus. The burden of moving becomes a two-day happening, with the movers sleeping on mattresses on the floor, communal meals at the local steak and pasta joint, humor and backbreaking work done with goodwill and some drama. It is actually fun. The kids and some of my friends join in, fascinated by Trip's nonstop monologues.

Bliss has moved into her own small one-bedroom apartment on Western Ave. near the river. Todd and I are sharing what had been the living room of the top-floor apartment. Boxes are piled high around our beds with paths in between for walkways. The kitchen will be gutted right away. I've bought a small fridge, which doubles as a night table. With that and the coffee machine at least we can make breakfast. Other meals will be takeout for a while.

It's exciting to see walls coming down, rooms enlarging, new windows bringing in light and fresh perspectives. The view from the back windows is over a series of gardens. A large maple poised in the third yard hides the apartment building to the left. Sun pours in on all sides. Across the street in the front is a row of 1900 brick town houses that look like Beatrix Potter in the city.

In the midst of all this my friend Rosemary calls and tells me to come to a workshop she is sponsoring. Rosemary lives in southern New Hampshire and has a yoga and movement studio. The class will be given by her daughter's closest friend, who went on to become a dancer performing in road versions of Broadway shows, but then left that to train in movement exploration and creative-arts therapy in San Francisco.

Jennifer is a tall willowy blond with a slow, warm smile. As she talks her body bends and moves, accompanying her words.

"Creative expression is a therapeutic approach in that it uses movement and the expressive arts in the process of revealing the self. We don't focus on pathology but on growth potential. This class will provide a space for you to go on a journey to explore both your wounds and your creative will. For every thought supported by feeling, there is a muscle change. Man's whole body records his or her emotional thinking. We're shaped according to those stories. Today we will move and draw in order to bring unconscious awareness into conscious expression."

Being in a spacious clean studio in the country on an early summer morning after the plaster-dust-and-cardboard-carton life in Cambridge gives me the willingness to dive into these exercises without my usual skepticism. First we are asked to draw our present life on large poster paper with crayons. Then it is suggested that we improvise with movement in response to what we drew. Finally we hunker down with pen and paper to write about what just happened. This is what I wrote:

As I danced my drawing there was a part that I moved to and a part I ignored. I wonder why? I want to know more. What does it mean to move, to react to my drawing? What have I learned? The drawing is a landscape, a small lake or pond with a boat and a bridge. In the foreground are shells.

The blue of the water. Blue water is my first choice always. What my eyes are drawn to, where I long to be. What I know. Why then do I fear water? Do I fear what I love best? Why do I fear that water will kill me? This is no mere fear of water. It is a deeper matter. It tugs and pulls and spirals into me. I did not dance the brown of wood, wood that is the bridge, wood that is the boat. I fear not breathing. Under the water I will drown. Underwater, overwhelmed. Does my life drown me? The green spirals that are meant to be the vegetation along the shore are really springs, like a Slinky gone awry. Coils of movement, taut, unexpected, jack-in-the-box. Then there are the clams and their darkness. I move like them. I am their hingeness, the opening and closing, the muscle without a thought, a brain, a word. No snapping words. The snapping can injure. Slow down the hinge. Slow down the opening and closing, and then the opening can expand and arch back to become a bridge. The stretching back over the fear, becoming the fear, writing my book, my fear, saying my words. This book, these words about grief, its blackness, its sadness, its sorrow is my bridge.

After drawing a picture of small amoeba shapes:

Who are you, little blobs, little pools of chaos? We are, I am, random cells, little messes, squiggly parts of you, tangled hair. Not to worry, we're little hair balls, we're innocent, innocent. Don't distrust us. We thrive on tangle, but it is our tangle. We like the frames you made, but we may push against them. Relax. Take it easy, love us. Don't tense up against us. See us as art, as decorations. Weave us into your soul.

This is the seductiveness of cancer.

To balance the disorder of Cambridge I continue my weekend commuting to Sandy Lodge. The animals, as do I, need their soft places, corners with cushions to snuggle into, to relax, to breathe dust-free air.

On the ferry I go up to the lunchroom for a hot dog and coffee and return to the car. I pick up a book but can't concentrate. My thoughts go to yesterday's wedding. I think of Anatole, wanting him with me as I go across to be with my new friends from the Mayo Clinic to whom I've lent the house, knowing how much he would have enjoyed these people. But what I'm really sad about is yesterday seeing Bliss watching her best friend from grade school walk down the aisle of a sun-filled church on the arm of her father.

As Anatole lay dying in the hospital, on those fifteen-minute morning drives back to keep watch, I would often think about how Bliss would have no father to walk her down the aisle on her wedding day, no one to give her away. Somehow this hurt the most, not that I was losing my companion, my lover, my best friend, but that our daughter would be stood up, abandoned at the altar, not by her intended, but by her parent. This ritual of a young woman being handed from one man to another, from the man whose passion and love begat her and whose passion and love cradled, coddled, cared for, protected, and held her for so many years, tradition prescribes that this older man, the father, hand to, give to a younger man this precious being, our daughter. This, Bliss will never have. She's been deserted by her father. I know that in her mind this is also an image for the future, the bride alone. Of course she will not be alone. Todd and I will be there to walk with her if she chooses, but in her mind as in mine there is the image of the woman in white alone, no arm to hold, to lean on. The balance and poise now must all be within herself, which they are. Her father's death has propelled this raven-haired beauty into the arms and caresses of her own talent.

I wonder if she would have been as aggressive about her own writing had her father lived. I have to be careful here in saying precisely what I mean, for I loathe the idea so current now that following pain and suffering there are gifts, rewards. That is not an axiom. Bliss had already begun writing in college. Her talent had surfaced before her father's death. I know from my own life that pain and loss only led to more pain and loss. After my parents died I spiraled down into alcohol and sleeping pills needing to dull and black out what was intolerable to bear.

There are still a few tears on these drives to Woods Hole. Not much and not for long. The misty eyes happen when I see a car loaded with a summer's worth of food, bikes, coolers, sleeping bags, plants, all the furnishings that accompany a family with children, dogs, cats in crates, water bowls. I realize the loss I feel is not just for Anatole's death but for the passing of those hectic nonstop days of children's squabbles, teenage babysitters, and no time for myself. I sit here on the freight deck in the car warmed by the early-morning summer heat, apart from the vacationers and families who line the upstairs decks to chatter, mingle, eat, and watch the gulls and shoreline of Woods Hole and the Elizabeth Islands slip by.

I purposely stay apart and separate. My mission is different. Not ease, pleasure, relaxation, but rather work. On my boat, my garden, my house, me. I am recrafting myself, reediting, redefining. Sometimes I wonder if I am going too far in this process, wanting or needing to make myself too special, too apart from what was familiar to me and my friends. I have become impatient and intolerant. Former pastimes no longer please. I am easily dismissive.

Passion and carnage interest me more than niceness and predictability. I'm living in a new house in Cambridge with no walls, no kitchen, torn-up bathrooms, but it is not uncomfortable. The plaster dust, shredded insulation, and dangling electric wires don't discourage me, pain me, the way these parked cars with family life do. I have been jolted into a track of my own making, which inflates my sense of self. I worry that I am digging too deeply, turning the track into a trench where dampness, isolation, and moisture and darkness breed their own brand of sickness and perversion. But to develop a perverted self is not altogether displeasing to me.

Baking a cake this afternoon at Sandy Lodge, I wonder about the nature of being connected to someone, a husband, my husband for twenty-nine years, now dead three years and eight months. I married at twenty-three and took that union for granted. Our connection was as solid, despite all our problems and conflicts, as the floor underneath our feet, the walls, the windows, the roof that sheltered us, the food we ate. It was a given. We worked on our marriage somewhat haphazardly. We worked at our jobs. We didn't feel we had to have a great marriage. We ended up with a reasonably good marriage. I never thought about who would die first, an amazing fact because Anatole was seventeen years older than I. His numerical age was never evident.

The twisting knife in my belly began when? Sometime this afternoon. Working in the garden after lunch, thinking I'll never go to the beach again. That used to be my recurring bad dream years ago. It would be August on the Vineyard and I hadn't gotten to the beach yet. This is happening. I don't want to go to the beach. I am a misfit there. Now I go to the beach alone. I no longer need a beach bag filled with towels, thermos, paddle rackets, a Frisbee. There's just me. All I need is a towel, perhaps a book. I feel such pressure to appear okay, to smile, to look successful, attractive, spirited, and yet I'm not, the knife pain pierces through my gut to keep a part of myself pinned to a dark place.

I want to be with another man and yet I can't imagine living with this in the presence of another. I now understand why Janis withdrew from all the friends she and Albert had when he died. There was no way she could continue to be two when she was reduced to one. She knew this and became her own one, withdrawing into her world of dogs and dog friends. She kept one friend from her former life, Helen, and that was all.

In my days now there is no soft cushion of time. No part of the day when, with a partner, you take a time-out, a walk perhaps, watch a TV show, go to a movie. If the dogs weren't here to walk and pet I'd go crazy. My days are driven, as I do lists of necessary things, and still I have no health insurance. Having had cancer I'm in a high-risk group and the HMOs won't touch me. Regular coverage is prohibitive in cost. My daughter accuses me of creating my own chaos. "Take responsibility for your life," she says. I just look at her as she says these words, my eyes becoming heavy. Yes, the deaths, the cancer, the complications of my brother's estate in Manchester, my small cat choked by cancer, losing the trees in the Vineyard, all my responsibility.

I was born. I have dared to breathe so that these hard things can occur in my life. There is a demand to be healed, this a desire from friends, an expectation from our culture. I want to scream, *Don't* make assumptions about my wounds. Let them be. Go on with your life and don't look, don't talk to me if what you find, what you see, is upsetting.

Recapitulation

Four years ago in July we would drive down to Woods Hole on Friday afternoons. There would be only a brief wait for a boat, forty minutes, perhaps an hour. We couldn't make reservations because we never knew if Anatole would feel well enough to travel, but often he would say that since he was feeling worse and worse, the Vineyard with sun and friends would be a better place to feel terrible.

Cambridge seemed abandoned that summer. Our phone sat quietly and no one rang the doorbell. Staying there made us feel as if our life was already over. On the Vineyard we would cling to the familiar settings and faces of happier times. Since all we'd known was bad luck that previous year, losing our furniture, poor health, I was always grateful for the brief wait, not having to spend precious hours on the asphalt lot. Anatole's impatience would have turned long hours of waiting into fury.

Today the wait is longer. President Clinton has begun to vacation here. Today's *Vineyard Gazette* announced his return. More national media for the island, more traffic, more tourists, longer waits.

On the freight boat I get out of my car, stand up by the rail, and watch for the gray-haired man in the red Peugeot whom I exchanged comments with as he joined the line some ten cars behind me. I pass him as I go through the hatch door to the forward deck. He doesn't see me. He is making a walking tour of the boat the way a nine-year-old child would. His license plate says Missouri. Perhaps this is his first crossing. The wind is blowing almost twenty knots. A forty-foot sloop, sails furled, motor on, is rocking like a hobbyhorse as she heads for Woods Hole. I watch her, wondering when she will bear off, as the freight boat and she have crossing paths.

A wave hits the bow and splashes over the railing. My head and chest are drenched with seawater and I can't open my eyes. A young girl behind me offers a towel. I take it with a smile, saying the salt water feels good. But I know my wet hair, now quite short, is dark and matted against my brow and that it accentuates the lines and austerity of my thin face in an unflattering way. I suddenly feel anger at myself for wanting to meet a man, for being hungry in that way. That kind of craving makes me feel like a sieve. The raw hunger for a man, hunger for an adventure, pierces holes in my selfhood. I lose shape and purpose, even though I don't have much idea of what my purpose might be.

If I can get the dogs to my boat, I will sleep on it tonight. I can hear Anatole's impatience and annoyance, telling me that this is a ridiculous plan. His worry often took the form of being annoyed. Coming to the island tonight—it is seven o'clock—I am homeless. My house is rented. Offers of a room from friends don't include the dogs, so I plan to sleep on the boat. It's a crazy thing to do and yet why not? It's a way to be separate and alone and that's what I want. My place, my space, my little house. Today driving down in the car I was talking to George and when I mentioned "little house" her tail started thumping. That's what we call her dog crate. If the thought of snugness, coziness, a familiar place to curl up in can give my dog George such pleasure, it's no wonder that I look forward to a small place of my own, a cuddy cabin, a floating nest.

Driving up-island I choose Middle Road. There is less traffic. The oak trees arch over the car, making a glimmering tunnel as light begins to fade. There on the town dock at Quitsa is my daughter, who knows of my plan and has decided to join me. The world's edges melt into softness lit by a multihued sky. We coax the dogs into the dinghy and row through the still water to *Swallow*, which is moored in the adjoining cove. Player jumps out once and we detour to a bank to get him back in the boat. Once settled we share the sandwiches, carrot sticks, and rice salad I have brought. Bliss and I have traveled back to my favorite childhood book, *Swallows and Amazons,* by Arthur Ransome, where children on an English lake spend the summer messing around in boats.

Back in Cambridge, a hard week. Annoyed at Rosemary, my good friend who feels she has to fix, offer a suggestion, make better. She tells me to eat something, to make a plan, to rest, to hire a cleaning woman. My anger is that she doesn't see that part of me that copes, that has always managed with the overloads in my life. She forgets my strengths. Yet by recounting the litany of recent disasters, I do invite her into the role of problem solver. The dogs peeing on the new wood floor, no lunch or dinner. I had told her of my fear of cancer returning. Why couldn't she have said, "God, you're really overwhelmed." I think because I'd frightened her.

On Tuesday, crying over the phone, I told her about my dream the night before. I was on the streets in a war-savaged neighborhood with three young children. There were ruined houses and rubble on street corners. There was no safety. Finally I got the children back to a hidden room that had been their home. I feared that their mother had been killed, but she was there asleep under blankets on a mattress on the floor. The small children, like puppies, crawled under the blankets to be with her and I sank onto the bare floor, heaving with grief, for I had no mother and have lived most of my life without a mother. I told the story of this dream to Rosemary along with all my other fears of instability, stress, an impecunious life. Will I lose Anatole's pension, my new Cambridge home? Earlier that morning I had been turned down once again for health insurance because I'd had cancer.

Seeing clients, going to dance class, finally a working sink in the kitchen, all this gets me through the week and eases my worries, but the city air is hot and heavy. Friday morning I pack up the animals and head down Route 3 to Woods Hole.

The ferry door, like a whale's jaw, slowly opens in front of me. I've stayed in my car while crossing. The brilliant blue of this cool September morning sweeps into the boat. These large-bellied boats seem like modern white whales. Like Jonah I will be glad to get out and go forward to this Labor Day Weekend. An American flag flies to the left of its pole, swept aloft by a brisk northwest wind cooling the summer sun. The President is here.

At work in Stoneham, I am with a patient who says, Every time I go to Faulkner Hospital I have to park in the garage.

Suddenly, an image of Dana Farber's garage. Entering the ramp, winding around. The concrete pillars, the asphalt floors. Never feeling afraid at midnight. The dim night light. The numbness. Leaving my husband every night. Is this memory or a flashback?

On the ferry to Oak Bluffs this morning there was an ambulance ahead of me in the center row. Five years ago an ambulance was called to the Martha's Vineyard Hospital to take my husband to Boston. I wonder if this was the day, September 23, and if this was the boat.

We had come down to the Vineyard for a weekend, to get away from the cancer, the hospital, and the home into which we'd moved seven weeks earlier. The move had been chaotic, with Anatole being diagnosed the following day. We couldn't get settled in the house. For many years we had both had the same recurring bad dream, which was that we'd bought the wrong house, a depressing house in a neighborhood that we realized was shabby only after we'd moved in.

It's strange that we'd both had this dream. Perhaps our experiences earlier in life had given us both a fear of displacement. Waking up in the wrong place, having lost what was familiar, a parent, a home. Our first home as children, whatever its flaws, was at least a home in which happiness could be hoped for, longed for.

Those ten days in August when my husband was told he had prostate cancer. "It's gone beyond the Rhine. It's probably in your lymph glands." That late-summer week when the moving company couldn't find one-third of our belongings. When we listened to all the cars and trucks that used our side street as a way to avoid Harvard Square traffic. When we found that to read the newspaper at breakfast, lights had to be turned on, for the house was heavily shaded by trees. In those early days of August we knew then that our dream about finding ourselves in the wrong house had come true. We should have been thankful for all those trees in a city, but we needed light.

Anatole had gone through a difficult diagnostic procedure in early September, a cystoscopy, which confirmed the initial examination that the cancer had spread beyond the prostate. There had been complications. A covering doctor had made his first house call in years because the postoperative follow-up and directions for care on leaving the hospital had been lax. Three weekends later we came to the Vineyard to reclaim some normalcy and to find the sun and ease that we'd not had that summer.

We arrived Friday night. Saturday morning Anatole did a few hours of work and then, late morning, we decided to do an easy jog, the two-mile loop around West Tisbury. Anatole felt well. His strength had returned. His legs were strong. We ran most of it. I was the one who lost my breath and had to walk a few times. Impatiently Anatole waited for me. It was a clear, sunny September day, the kind of perfect day that seems to happen only on the Vineyard. We went home and had lunch. An hour later the pain began. Anatole had been thirsty after the run and had drunk a lot of water. An hour later he found he couldn't pee, only a few drops of blood. The pressure began to build up in his bladder and turned into a piercing pain. We headed down-island to the emergency room. I remember driving the long straight stretch of Old County Road, Anatole doubled over in pain, asking, pleading with me to drive faster. I had never seen him or anyone else folded over, sucked out, inverted in that way by physical pain. Not even the grimness on my father's face as he lived through the skeletal pain of multiple myeloma equaled the anguish in my husband's voice and posture.

Five years later I am sitting at the desk in his study writing these words. There is a nor'easter, rain with strong winds tugging at the trees outside, water gurgling down gutters, water coming in waves, unleashed forces of nature. Secure and dry in this wooden house I wonder about the physical pain of that day for my husband. Like the water overflowing the gutters and spilling down the sides of this house, the pain came too fast. Waves of raw sensation, brutal in their course, forced Anatole to lose his hold, literally his grip on himself. Anatole, the man of style, of wit, of grace, torn from himself by the searing agony, the deluge of pain that is beyond imagination, and yet I was there, inches away from his body, terrified, helpless, pressing on the accelerator, eyes switching back and forth from the road to Anatole to the road to Anatole, stifling screams that were rising in my throat, screams for help, screams to tell the world that my husband was being killed. Stop it. Stop it. Help him. My God, *Stop It!* Screaming at the pain as if it were embodied, a physical assailant. If this had been a dream I might have woken up. I often wake up at unbearable parts in a dream. But in life you don't wake up. There *is* no way to get away, to get out.

At the hospital, finally, with a combination of medical procedures, nerve-numbing pain injections, and compassionate nurses, the pain was caught and caged, but the pacing animal that it was refused to leave my husband's body, so the next morning an ambulance was called. Perhaps it had come over on the 9:45 a.m. boat like the one I saw today. Anatole and I left the island on the twelve-noon boat, he in an ambulance half-conscious, the dogs and I following in the gray van. He was drained by a solid twenty hours of catheters being pumped out to clear the urethra of clots of tissue that were breaking away from a not yet healed bladder that had been sliced apart for the biopsy. Perhaps the cancer had already rotted that tissue.

After an event of illness there are so many distortions, at least there are in my mind, as to what had really happened inside my husband's body. These are my thoughts.

When the first doctor said the word *cancer* to my husband, at that moment like the leaves of the sensitive plant that fold into themselves when touched, perhaps the tissues and cells around the prostate gland shrank back in horror and in fear. They held their breath, they turned blue. They forgot what they were supposed to do, these cells, especially when a searching scalpel cut into the sanctity of their place. They lost their bearings. They wilted, shriveled, and in losing their shape, just like my husband who lost his shape with the pain, they lost their grip, that way they had of holding on to one another so that in the tissue of the bladder those frightened cells, emptied of spirit, full of panic, minute bits of the man I loved, the man I depended on, the man I needed, began to rot, to soften. They gave up. Perhaps they mistook the jarring impact of the running for another incision, another assault on their sanctity, so they lost their nerve. They could no longer cling, no longer cleave to one another. They began to fall apart, and the moisture and motion of that sudden reversal became the blood and clots that choked my husband's urethra. The centrifugal life-supporting flow of our bodies moving always toward our centers, our hearts, our desires, our passions, had stopped. Like refugees dropping their belongings and scattering every which way when a bomber flies in low, spraying machine-gun bullets, these cells panicked and left their rightful place. They became aimless, homeless, the pattern, the direction of their lives destroyed. This is how I understand cancer.

This morning, October 11, waking up at seven, remembering, crawling back into bed. Huddled. The phone call. Waiting to wake Bliss. Calling Todd. Going to the hospital. Remembering my own father's death. Waking up in the morning. Being told. The dining room empty. Grandfather died in a dining room. The calls to the undertaker.

Later in the day, memories of four years ago are more defined. On that morning I'd been woken from a deep sleep by the phone ringing at 6:30 a.m., and then the soft, slow voice of a nurse, Alma, telling me that Anatole was gone. I can't remember the exact word the Dana Farber nurses used to speak of death. They didn't say *dead* or *he died*. They said something else. Something else that was milder, softer, referring to a transition rather than a break. They chose words to soothe. This soft-skinned woman, I remember she had a fair, glowing complexion and dark blond hair, this nurse, Alma, who all night had been tending to my husband, monitoring his vital signs, counting his breaths, called me and woke me. She had waited a half hour. Anatole died at six. Alma called at six-thirty. She called to tell me in slow, calm, measured phrases that my husband had died, or did she say departed? I asked her how, what had happened that was different. I had thought he had another few days, that we would have more time with me hovering and Anatole drifting more deeply into a coma, his final punctuation—a long, struggling, silent pause before the end of his life. I would kiss his brow, whispering, My baby, my baby. For in some sense dying had returned him to his infancy. The expression on his face, in his eyes, the trusting helplessness was that of a baby who can't move, can't raise his head.

Barely awake. My breath and questions matched the carefully measured breaths and pauses of Alma as she told me that during the night Anatole's breaths had slowed, slowed down to only four each minute, and then between 4 and 6 a.m. they had slowed even further, until at six my husband's lungs stopped moving. Later in the day I wondered if the nurses had just slightly increased the morphine as a gentle way of soothing, supporting his moving on. I remember the word now they used for dying. It was *pass*.

Such presumption on their part. Passing on to what, where? My husband's dying was no slight shift of place. It was a shock, a tragedy, a fracturing of so many of our dreams, our assumptions, our future. The fact of my husband's death, anyone's death, calls for the chords of a grand Bach cantata, the stomp and blare of a New Orleans jazz funeral, not the silent, stealth-like, smooth-seamed sound of a word like *pass*. Please pass the butter. The offertory plate gets passed in church. These are horizontal actions. A football pass has an arc, but the ball lands again. Death is not horizontal. There is no arc that returns to earth. The fact of death the moment you learn, know that someone you love has died, if one was to choose a word implying movement, it might be that death is a shattering, or explosion, annihilation. The anima of the physical body is gone, never to return. Gone. The flesh is still. Blood no longer flows. There is a rip, a tear, a break so sudden and large and final that you lose your breath, your reality, your feelings.

Eighty cars ahead of me in Woods Hole on a Friday night, mid-October. The standby line has been closed. I will have to wait for a morning boat. Overnighters are being directed to the far side of the terminal. Player frantically leans out of the car window sniffing the sea air, blocking conversation with the Steamship Authority attendant.

Here I've been, quietly staying in my car with the three animals on this temperate fall night, surrounded by other travelers. I get a cheeseburger and apple juice and come back to the car to eat my dinner in darkness. The meal makes me sleepy, so I lower the back of the seat and curl up with a sweatshirt for a pillow. As I was leaving Boston on Route 3, crawling southward with evening traffic, overhead, coming in for final approach, was a procession of planes, landing gear down, slowing down for the descent into Logan Airport. Two were jumbo jets, perhaps from Europe, moving at a lumbering pace, awkward and fragile, filled with people all with their stories, their dramas, and then myself, only one of a broad stream of slow-moving cars, each driver with a destination, a purpose, a place, a plan. All this moving of humanity late on a Friday. My destination today seems less clear, less focused, more ordinary. I want less. I feel less. The pain and tears have worn off my sharp edges. Words no longer spill from me.

Unpacking

The phone rang last night while I was eating a late dinner. My son's voice, breathless, was assuring me that he was all right. There was a fire across the street from where he was working, installing an alarm system in a hair salon. The biggest fire he'd ever seen. He was concerned that I might see the report of the fire on the evening news and worry about him. As he talked he could see the buildings, two wooden triple-deckers with bow fronts, vintage Cambridge, engulfed in flames that soared above the roofs. I asked Todd if he was in a safe place. He reassured me that he was. I hung up, finished my supper, and was absentmindedly watching television when I began to hear the sirens of fire trucks passing through my neighborhood on their way to Inman Square, an area of Cambridge that is crowded with wooden houses, shoulder to shoulder. The flames my son had described I now imagined spreading down rows of houses, leaping across streets. I became frightened for his safety.

I had to park the car a half mile away. For blocks there was an endless line of fire trucks, canvas hoses snaking along streets. A river of runoff water six feet wide had formed by the curb. Turning the corner into Cambridge Street, I saw the two burning buildings. Fire trucks parked at angles had their ladders extended toward the blaze and were pumping water onto the roofs. Across the street was the hair salon where my son was working. The owner of the store had been the first to notice the fire and had called the fire department. There were rumors on the street that it might have been arson. Rent control had just that week been repealed by vote in Cambridge, and these had been rent-controlled houses.

Waking up this morning, I panicked on finding Todd's bed empty. When I left Inman Square he was finishing up the alarm installation. I came home and went straight to bed and assumed he did the same and would sleep in a bit. When I saw that he wasn't in his room, I became apprehensive, my crazy mind suddenly convinced that he'd not come home, that he was hurt or dead. I hadn't known that he had to get to a job site south of Boston by seven-thirty.

Today, this morning, walking from dance class to my car, I thought about all the losses of the people whose homes were in flames. On the news one person said it was only stuff. She could replace it all. That's not my way. I can't replace any of what has left me. I can't replace my husband, my brother, my former life, my son. This morning when my paranoia was overshadowing me, I sensed once again how thin my skin is. I have never been able to see violent movies or horror films. If I did past-life therapy I would probably be told that I had lost my husband and all five children during a war, or we were massacred by Indians as we crossed the plains. I doubt that this information would ease my sensitivity to suffering. I realized today with great clarity that I wouldn't want to diminish my capacity to feel pain, to worry, my readiness for panic. They are all responses to real things that are happening to a real me in a very real life. It would dishonor, diminish the loss, the tragedy of death if I were to find a way to lighten my heart.

Last night on the eleven o'clock news the weather forecast was for unseasonably high temperatures through the weekend. Warming to the fifties, possibly the sixties. Earlier this week we'd had our first real snow, five inches, and now a return of mild weather. There is a lot of painting and paperwork for me to do in Cambridge, but I crave long views and the isolation of nature. I know if I stayed in Cambridge I'd be aching for the Vineyard, so this morning I called my builder and made an appointment to meet with him on Saturday at noon. My brother's estate has finally been settled, and there are just enough funds to add a winterized addition to Sandy Lodge. For years, even before Anatole got sick, I have daydreamed about an annex to the summerhouse. One room downstairs. A bedroom and study above.

Sixty degrees on a Saturday morning in January. A couple is walking down Abel's Hill in shorts. Warm air, bare trees, bare legs. John Novak, with whom Todd worked during college summers, comes by at midday to talk about possibilities. There is a small rise to the southeast of the summerhouse, a tree in between. Whatever is built needs to be an addition, as my deed prohibits a separate guest house. We realize that the two buildings—the tree dictates an eighteen-foot separation—can be connected by an arbor or, if need be, a breezeway. I know I am stretching the definition of an "addition." John and I talk numbers. Perhaps we can start this spring.

Marcus has noticed that I'm not okay. He called yesterday. I've been getting to only two or three classes a week. I hadn't been calling him. I usually do just to keep in touch. The phone rang. I was surprised by his voice. Any voice would have surprised me. I'd spent three days by myself painting, finishing the wall glazing in my bedroom, and then beginning the walls of the back stairs. By the lower steps a peachy-rose wash of color melds into a soft blue-green, wisps of color easing the transition from the fire of the just-appearing sun to the blue of the sky overhead. Why a sunrise on the stairwell to my bedroom? Now, with the leaves off the trees, in this new house, these are the colors I see at dawn. This gaudy painted sky is the backdrop for the trellis and plants I will create with stencils that will join the plants that are already sitting on the stair landing under the two skylights there.

This nonstop painting project has pulled me into a place of stillness where my aloneness surfaces and begins to ask questions. The inquisition distorts me.

Marcus notices my half-choked voice, my incomplete sentences. He knows something is troubling me. I don't know how to explain it. I suggest to him that it's the ongoing disruptions of the renovation, or conversely it may be that now the work is almost done, I sense that I'll miss the sociability and friendliness of the crew when they're gone.

I am living in a place that Anatole never saw, did not help to choose or arrange. Being here on Frost Street is entirely my own doing. I don't go on about this with Marcus. I switch the topic. We talk about his worries. I hang up and go back to work.

Later in the week I return to these thoughts of a new home and my current unease. As the slow unpacking proceeds from the jumble of cardboard boxes in the basement, with the sorting, the decisions about what to keep, what to use, what to store for later, I realize I must do this unpacking and sorting where it most matters. Inside of myself.

I have moved away from Anatole, moved into my own life. The distance is now between Sandy in her late fifties, struggling to shape a life, and Sandy for twenty-nine years a young matron and then a less-young matron, mother of two children, volunteer in various cultural activities, gardener, furnisher of antique homes. Sandy the wife of an interesting man, a writer. Sandy the part-time dance teacher, sometime performer. Then Sandy the social work student, and finally Sandy the therapist. I had this life, fully crafted, which was often unwieldy to carry, but it was dense, solid with demands, occasional dinner parties, old friends, new friends, even a sailboat. I had come to realize in my forties that I was blessed with my life and that I was a happy person. Then we moved to Cambridge and this new chapter began.

When Anatole was sick we had many moments and even some days of happiness. Today, my animals, a phrase in dance class, a walk on a Vineyard beach can make me happy. Yet as I look into myself, as I stand still as I did this weekend while painting, the deeper places of myself rise up and they bring sadness. This is an evolving sadness that is not so much the pain of Anatole's suffering and death but rather about this ontological shift in my life.

Ontological was a word that Anatole used a bit too frequently in his book reviews of the seventies. In his defense, he was an ontological kind of guy. The word fit him. It put a jazzy spin, with its five-syllable syncopation, on his restlessness. Ontology is the study of what exists. Who am I? What is the nature of my being?

With Anatole I had a role, a context, a fully furnished, almost Victorian life in its absence of empty space. There was a sense of a future. Travel, friends, work continuing, more time for ourselves, grandchildren one day. Now I am single, fifty-seven, a widow. I work part-time as a therapist. I go to dance classes to stay in shape. I take care of three animals. I try to take care of myself. I talk to friends on the phone more than I see them. I have drifted away from social scenes. I see an occasional movie. I am not a significant other. My significance must be, needs to be, to myself. The problem is that the sadness and the aloneness thin out that significance and I end up feeling and behaving in arbitrary ways.

These feelings are not simply the signs of a depression—they tell of a deeper and darker shift, a disengagement from a part of myself and how I was anchored in life with all those necessary things and chores I did for family and home. Now the demands come only from me, and I sense that I'm sliding into the guise of a philosopher, living at a distance, leaning back in a chair, slumped to one side, chin in hand, eyeing my life, instead of rolled-up sleeves at the kitchen sink, shouting that dinner is ready.

I wasn't always happy with Anatole. He could be selfish, insensitive, unkind, impatient. There would be hours and an occasional day when I'd be very angry at him for his less-than-perfect partnering. But the anger and the energy of strong feeling was as much of an attachment to him and to our life as were the happy, silly, tender times. For years I'd lived the drama of a very complicated duet, and now I am doing a solo with hesitant and awkward choreography.

I have designed and arranged this new home. It is turning out well. This is a fine space in which to live. That is all to the good. Perhaps I'm being too hard on myself. I probably need time now to relax, finish the unpacking, finish the painting, and take some deep breaths even though they hurt.

I had been out of sorts that Sunday morning. Two workshops the day before. One on family intimacy and the other on survival and mortality. Saturday night I felt alone and flat. Sunday morning was not much better. I had no motivation to begin any of the painting chores around the house. I thumbed through the *Boston Globe*, past articles that seemed too boring even to scan. I found myself on the last page of the Arts section, the page that has the personal ads.

Even though two friends of mine have married men they met through a personal ad I have always thought that resorting to this way of meeting someone was a desperate gesture, a naked admission of need, of an incompleteness, a hunger. God forbid that anyone should know, that even I should know, that I am on the outside wanting to get in. I've always indulged in the smugness of staying in whatever mess I've found myself in and declaring the dilemma to be a drama, a way station on my circuitous path through life. This particular Sunday I sensed the pall of the dead-end place of living alone, working long days with a minimal social life. I wanted new information. I needed a rash act.

I've often looked over the personal columns, women looking for men, men looking for women, men looking for men. I've read them as an anthropologist, a commentator on the human condition. Once I'd even gone so far as to call and hear the voices of the men who placed these ads. The three I chose all sounded like furniture salesmen from southern New Hampshire. This morning, because I was curious, I called two. One had not recorded a message. The other, an ad stating "moving on, shifting horizons, wish to see the world anew," did have an aural counterpart. I heard a voice saying something about what that person had done that day. I didn't listen to the words. I heard the resonance, the timbre, the breath behind and within the sound. Not thinking about what I was doing I left a brief message and thought, Oh well. So what? But my heart was lighter.

Later that night the phone rang. A man's voice, saying, "You answered my ad."

We talked for an hour. We spoke about the aesthetic of having no endings. We agreed to meet in nine days' time for lunch at the French Patisserie in Harvard Square. That was four weeks ago.

It occurred to me in the nine days of waiting that there was a possibility that this man could become more than a friend, that something very wonderful could come into my life. After all of the sadness and sorrow of the past five years, what happens all the time to so many people in this world, meeting and falling in love, could also happen to me. Such a common everyday occurrence. There are couples everywhere. All shapes and sizes.

I had gone to bookstores the first year after Anatole died and browsed through "widow books," trying to find information on how to do it, how to lead this new life, how to be a widow. I would leaf through to the back pages and find the part about how this woman met her new love, her second husband. As with sex scenes in a racy book, I was curious and also a little disgusted. How could these women after nine months, after a year, even two years, give themselves up to the embrace of another man, sell their souls, step away from their grief, disfigure their loss by trading it away for a new affection. Inside, what means did they have to connect with anyone else? Weren't they still in shreds? Was the new, posttrauma relationship a gloss-over, a makeover, a make-do, a defense against the suction of the infinite, as Ernest Becker says in *The Denial of Death*? That's what it looked like, and my prideful soul, my erect dancer's back, would have none of it.

Four years and seven months now since Anatole died. Years filled with work; two books published, a social work practice established, a new home, and training my body to move once more as a dancer moves, writing these pages, using these words, braiding them, weaving them into a tether to lead me through the pain, loss, and angry sadness. I am in a new place now, moving on.

It's 8:40 p.m. and I'm on a freight boat in Vineyard Sound, a cluster of cars on a stubby barge chugging its way around the entrance buoy for Woods Hole harbor. To my right the final glow of dull, somber rose fading into a dark azure outlines the Elizabeth Islands with black. The engine slows to half speed. Soon the ferry will turn, aiming its mouth toward its berth. The lines will be tossed and secured, the canvas gate drawn back, and once more I will head north to Cambridge, but this time when I get home I can make a call and there will be a voice asking, How was your drive, how was your day? Someone waiting to hear from me.

Left Cambridge after three hours' sleep. Got here at 7:30 and was the third car in the fourth row. There are always a lot of trucks on Friday, so I knew there'd be a minimum three- to four-hour wait. This line, cars parked end to end in close formation, is a refuge, a familiar place, an alternate home for me. A place to be safe, giving me time to stop and consider. In all kinds of weather I sit in the car with my animals and look at myself, my behavior, take my emotional pulse as I find words and sentences that tell me and reveal to me what I don't see during my busy week.

My plan for today was to have driven down late this afternoon to get across tonight, but instead I woke up early and knew I had to leave. This new man in my life and I had spent some time together last night. Like noxious gases rising, our fears and mutual ambivalence came to the surface. We both pulled back, then tried to reach for each other, only to grasp empty air. We had talked about his helping me with the drawings for the addition yesterday, but when I woke this morning all I could do was flee, get out of town, before sunup, as in an old, grainy black-and-white western. I left in the early half-light, moving silently, heading beyond the foothills of the suburbs to the narrow canyons of parked cars in standby, where I could settle down and rest, regroup and reconsider.

I am suddenly critical and negative about those things that I found so charming in my new friend only a few days ago. I fear that my need to hold and in turn to be held inflates my affections, that I mistake the tumescence of desire for the beginnings of love. I worry that the scarring in my life has placed me beyond the possibility of any relationship. The new man suggested that I might not yet be ready for a relationship. What if this is true? If I'm not capable of a relationship now, will I ever be? I've done my homework. I've been present with my grief. I have acted out my impulsiveness. I have ordered my house. Why such a narrow eye in the needle? What more do I have to do to get to the other side—the place of companionship, love, partnership, home?

This reminds me of the dilemma of faith, that it requires a decision, an action, the existential leap of the Danish philosopher. There is so much about the new man that is wonderful, that fits, that attracts, that would wear well. I don't want to be flippant and toss him away because of my inconsistencies, my unpredictability. I wonder about my capacity, my desire for stability, for a new relationship. This writing, something I never did while Anatole was alive, keeps a part of Anatole present in me. An observing, commenting voice that I listened to for twenty-nine years is now lodged in my heart, my consciousness. Does this demand an independent life? Anatole was curious about the world. Always there was his need to explore, find the new. Does this have to be kept alive in me, this Broyard family tradition of the boulevards, the wandering, exploring? No, the restlessness was for Anatole an unhappy driven behavior, a faulty solution to unresolved issues of his own childhood. Conversely, the writing was his genius, the reinvention of himself and his world, a re-creation, reincarnation of his disappointments and desires. So the writing I will hold on to, the wanderlust not.

The solution of course is to move slowly. My being wants to race, cut to the chase, find the resolution one heartbeat after the beginning. I want the surprise and drama of a sudden romance, an intense connection, the swoop and fall of passion that lands on a commitment for life. Arrow, darts, hearts and cupids, swift passage slicing through air finding the mark, the bull's-eye. But sitting here I know that what I really want is something that has taken time to grow. All I can do now is know that I am confused.

Today there is a rally meeting of Corvettes on the island. Late and older models, convertibles, hardtops, sleek, jazzy, low-slung, white, red, black, and gray sports cars bringing glamour to the parking lot. Each car comes with a couple. Did they all struggle to find each other? Can I ask them?

Mother's Day today. A weekend alone at Sandy Lodge. I was relieved to be alone, glad that the new man had not come. I can sift through myself, pay attention to the internal swellings and contractions of aloneness, need, distance, desire, and disregard. I see in these past five days how much I am pulling away from something real, something steady, something that I say I want. I am embarrassed about introducing a new person into my life. What does the fact that I am attracted to this man say about me? And why wouldn't I want my friends to know more about me. They already know so much. It may be that the contact with the new man is revealing something that I do not want to know or see, something that I'm willing to shun, live without, something about touching, being close. I don't want to be a public failure, so I don't want others to know about this. This is where I get lost, in these thoughts. I just don't know what I think or feel about this man except that I want to see him.

Today, late in the afternoon, just before leaving Sandy Lodge, I was looking at the plantings up against the house, trying to judge how much to cut them back. Through the day I had been thinking about how it would be if this man were here with me. Whether it would feel right or be awkward. Bliss had just called to wish me Happy Mother's Day. Could I imagine him meeting my daughter, being with her? No, that's just too intimate. At that moment a bird flew into the plate glass of the kitchen window. A sharp metallic thud and it dropped to the ground. I gasped and was shocked into stillness. I know birds can be spirits. I clearly heard Anatole saying, "Get over it. I'm dead. See. Thud. Splat. I'm gone. For God's sake get on with your life."

By late August this new man and myself are parted. The ambivalence was greater than the connection. We had some marvelous times together. The ending was quick and neat.

Continuing

There is a piece by William Saroyan that was reprinted in the *New York Times* in their series of writers on writing, "Starting with a Tree and Finally Getting to the Death of a Brother." He recommends beginning with a specific object, "those companions of this place, each fixed into the soil of where it is." These perceivable things, Saroyan says, will then lead us by way of association, memory, and daydreams through the dim halls and unfolding horizons of our particular existence, embracing along the way its sorrow and joy. This is Saroyan's answer to his question "How do you die, write, live, sicken, heal, despair, rejoice?"

I have begun this effort of placing words on paper with the death of my husband and have now arrived at a pale yellow water lily with its unblemished petals facing the sun. Opposite in direction from Saroyan's advice, but I am not a writer by trade and for me this is the only story that has brought pencil to paper, this story of loss and living.

Six years ago I stopped scribbling in notebooks as I waited for the ferry. I don't remember how or why, perhaps I had begun to make reservations and no longer had the protracted waits in standby. Perhaps I turned instead to the daily paper or a book. Now, having finally joined the cell phone generation, I return phone messages while I wait in Woods Hole.

In these years I have moved to the Vineyard. The winterized addition became a reality. John Novak and I improvised a plan, making adjustments as we went along. A living room with a half kitchen in one corner. A Norwegian cupboard bed in another adjoins a sunroom. Upstairs there is a study alcove, bath, and bedroom, sufficient space for Vineyard winters. As spring warms I move back to the original uninsulated part of the house—or summer wing, as I now call it. I am here on the Vineyard year round.

Behind the winter wing there was a spot of level land, which gave way to a southeastern slope. This grassy area near the house seemed to be a good place for a terrace. I dug two rectangular plots and planted small box hedges and perennial flowers. Right angles here near the house in deference to David Hicks, the English designer who disdains free-form borders, decreeing that their oozing shapes must, if they are to be used at all, be at some distance from the balanced symmetry of ninety-degree walls and windows.

Hicks was right. This small nod to formality works, surveying as it does the descending field with woods beyond. Something more was needed, however, a transition from the exactness of geometry to the random patterns of nature. With the help of a bobcat, a small fishpond was dug, an oval seven feet across and two feet in depth. Bliss and a friend lugged rocks to surround the pond after we lined it with heavy vinyl. I bought a few aquatic plants at a local nursery. Time supplied the rest.

Late August of the first summer a fish appeared, a flash of orange glinting between the fernlike foliage of the water plants. The pond froze solid for a few weeks in the coldest part of the winter, and I feared for its lone inhabitant. The following summer there were four fish. A frog appeared the third summer. I read a bit about ponds and learned about feeding fish, and added a small circulating pump and a floating heating disk for winter, which keeps an area of water unfrozen. Now there are two frogs, five large fish, and twenty small ones.

Early June of this past year round leaves began to form near the base of the statue, a small concrete boy holding a fish, that sits off-center in the pond. As summer continued, the leaves grew larger, and one day in mid-August there was a perfectly formed pale-yellow water lily. The buds begin by nosing up between the leaves. You don't notice them until they spread their petals and reach for light and warmth. Like morning glories they close at night.

I saw the first water lily on a morning when I was overly busy with preparing my house and yard for a two-week rental. I'd not rented for five years, but had to now because the house needed a new roof and some other repairs, which the rental income would cover. This particular morning I was out of sorts, feeling quite sorry for myself that I was caught up in the nonstop work of cleaning out closets, drawers, kitchen cabinets on a day with a cloudless blue sky and an easy breeze that would have made a beach walk or boat excursion memorable. Instead there was this yellow flower, attended by a frog on a lily pad like a drawing in a children's book, depicting a magical scene in nature, a place of delight. What I'm trying to describe is that sense of discovery that young children have as they explore their back yards, the nearby woods, the shallow edge of a lake or pond, and see something new, something surprising that is there for their eyes only and sparks their curiosity and gives them great pleasure.

It is a mystery as to how these water lily plants came to thrive in my little pond. Fish eggs were probably mixed in with those few plants I purchased the first year. This might be true of the water lilies, except the local nursery where I bought the plants doesn't carry water lilies. Would a bird or insect have carried a seed? Could it have been the wind?

The water lilies have continued to bloom, new blossoms

opening every few days, on into early fall. Each one gives me intense pleasure, and each one tells me that life can save us with its beauty and the art we create, for these are Georgia O'Keeffe flowers, which have struggled, their buds pushing up through the murky water to air and light to open.

These flowers, their unbidden appearance, their perfection and glory, are a metaphor, a reminder, a tap on the shoulder that shows me again and again the radiance of being alive.

C. S. Lewis's classic book about grieving the loss of his wife is titled *Surprised by Joy,* and this is what I have experienced with these pale, floating buttercream flowers. They tell me that I don't know what will appear in my life, what my senses will experience, what my life will be. They tell me to look, taste, smell, listen, feel, so as not to miss what is possible. Again lines from Wallace Stevens:

The greatest poverty is not to live
In a physical world, to feel that one's desire
Is too difficult to tell from despair.

Life these past six years on the Vineyard has been good, hard at times, but mostly good. I have a small psychotherapy practice, volunteer in a community project, and continue dancing and even performing each winter with Vineyard Dance, a group of eighteen or so women. We are all students of Bill Costanza. We choreograph our own dances, translating our desires and fears, feelings, thoughts, and impulses into space, time, and shape. For four nights in late January the Vineyard Playhouse is filled with responsive audiences. Each of us knows that what we do together in creating these performances is important and soul-binding. For us, to one another, and to those who watch.

That first winter, six years ago, I began to work with all the words that had filled five notebooks and various scraps of paper written in standby, in spaces between clients, and on lone weekends. I deciphered the longhand scrawls and typed them into my computer. I joined a writing group and read through the material raw. The West Tisbury Library sponsored a writing workshop with a teacher from Boston. All those pages needed to be edited, shaped, formed, mined for an internal logic that would extend their meaning beyond myself. It seemed hopeless. Each morning I would turn on my computer before starting the day. From six to eight I would read and edit, reread and edit. I did not begin with a tree but I knew I had to be specific. Beginning to move through the manuscript blindly, as in a room before dawn, I found my way by reaching out for what was solid. The real things, the places, the events, the sensations, those flagships in our memory are what guided me in the quiet morning hours at my desk.

There have been months that I've not looked at these pages, other concerns being front and center, but I've known that shaping words is essential to continuing with my life. Being alive means telling one's story, be it to a friend, a priest, a therapist, or a journal. Writing at the beginning of a day is how I have become aware of where I am, where I have been. I am less caught in false assumptions as words spread out before me. Loss and grief can burrow in and not let go. These words have kept me breathing, helped me to examine my feelings, and to know that these many years later I have lived with and through the loss, so that now I can distinguish ordinary dissatisfaction and disappointment from grief, and that I can be freely happy when I'm dancing or with a friend or discovering a butter-hued water lily.

I have not remarried, nor am I living with a man, but there are men in my life who are good friends, close friends. At times I would like a partner, but I also appreciate my independence. I've come to know that I am passionate about being on the water, being near the water, so I have become an avid fisherman, getting a twenty-two-foot bass boat with a home-improvement loan from a local bank that understands these things. The boat has a dark-blue hull and a new inboard motor, and as she came to me nameless, her stern now says *Amazon,* the other half of the duo in Arthur Ransome's children's book. *Swallow,* my catboat, finally got in the water again this year and they are moored some twenty yards apart in a protected cove in Quitsa Pond here in Chilmark.

To be off Gay Head or in Robinson's Hole when fish are breaking, casting to their frenzy, or wading at Dog Fish Bar as the sun is setting with fish swirls around your feet, a fly line in your hand, is a moment of exquisite pleasure. I think of it as being at a fish party—the motion, the attentiveness of fish and fisherman. I crimp my barbs and release the fish, so life can go on.

A Note on the Type

This book was set in Adobe Garamond. Designed for the Adobe Corporation by Robert Slimbach, the fonts are based on types first cut by Claude Garamond (c. 1480–1561). Garamond was a pupil of Geoffroy Tory and is believed to have followed the Venetian models, although he introduced a number of important differences, and it is to him that we owe the letter we now know as "old style." He gave to his letters a certain elegance and feeling of movement that won their creator an immediate reputation and the patronage of Francis I of France.

Composed by Creative Graphics,
Allentown, Pennsylvania
Printed and bound by R. R. Donnelley & Sons,
Harrisonburg, Virginia
Designed by Anthea Lingeman